AVIS AU PUBLIC

Faire de la bonne cuisine demande un certain temps. Si on vous fai
c'est pour mieux vous servir, et vous plaire.

S0-ADG-935

ENTREES (SUITE)

Côtelettes d'agneau grillées 2.00

Côtelettes d'agneau aux champignons frais 2.25

Filet de boeuf aux champignons frais 4.25

Ris de veau à la financière 1.75

Filet de boeuf nature 3.50

Tournedos Médicis 3.00

Pigeonneaux sauce paradis 3.00

Tournedos sauce béarnaise 3.00

Entrecôte minute 2.50

Filet de boeuf béarnaise 3.75

Tripes à la mode de Caen (commander d'avance) 1.75

Entrecôte marchand de vin 3.75

Côtelettes d'agneau maison d'or 2.25

Côtelettes d'agneau à la parisienne 2.25

Foies de volaille à la brochette 1.50

Tournedos nature 2.50

Filet de boeuf à la hawaïenne 3.75

Tournedos à la hawaïenne 3.00

Tournedos marchand de vin 3.00

Pigeonneaux grillés 2.75

Entrecôte nature 3.50

Châteaubriand (30 minutes) 6.50

LÉGUMES

Epinards sauce crème .60

Broccoli sauce hollandaise .80

Pommes de terre au gratin .60

Haricots verts au beurre .60

Petits pois à la française .60

Chou-fleur au gratin .60

Asperges fraîches au beurre .90

Carottes à la crème .60

Pommes de terre soufflées .60

SALADES

Salade Antoine .60

Salade Mirabeau .75

Salade laitue au roquefort .80

Salade de légumes .60

Avocat Antoinette .75

Salade de laitue aux tomates .60

Salade d'anchois 1.00   Avocat à la vinaigrette .60

Fonds d'artichauts Bayard .90

Salade de laitue aux oeufs .60

Tomate frappée à la Jules César .60

Salade de coeur de palmier 1.00

Salade aux pointes d'asperges .60

DESSERTS

Gâteau moka .50

Méringue glacée .50

Crêpes Suzette 1.25

Soufflé au chocolat (2) (40 minutes) 2.00

Soufflé à la vanille (2) (40 minutes) 2.00

Glace sauce chocolat .50

Fruits de saison à l'eau-de-vie .75

Omelette soufflée à la Jules César (2) 2.00

Cerises jubilé 1.25

Crêpes à la gelée .80

Crêpes nature .70

Omelette au rhum 1.10

Glace à la vanille .40

Fraises au kirsch .90

Pêche Melba .60

Omelette Alaska Antoine (2) 2.50

FROMAGES

Roquefort .50

Camembert .50

Liederkranz .50

Gruyère .50

Fromage à la crème Philadelphie .50

CAFÉ ET THÉ

Café .15

Café brulôt diabolique 1.00

Café au lait .15

Thé glacé .15

Thé .15

Demi-tasse .10

EAUX MINERALES—BIERE—CIGARES—CIGARETTES

White Rock

Perrier

Vichy

Bière locale

Cliquot Club

Cigares

Cigarettes

Canada Dry

Roy L. Alciatore, Propriétaire

713-717 Rue St. Louis   Nouvelle Orléans, Louisiane

NEW ORLEANS

Classic

CREOLE

RECIPES

Paul Rico

NEW ORLEANS *Classic* CREOLE RECIPES

From Favorite Restaurants

KIT WOHL

FOREWORD BY CHRIS ROSE

PELICAN PUBLISHING COMPANY

Gretna 2014

ISBN 9781455618798

E-book ISBN 9781455618804

Printed in China
Published by Pelican Publishing Company, Inc.
1000 Burmaster Street, Gretna, Louisiana 70053

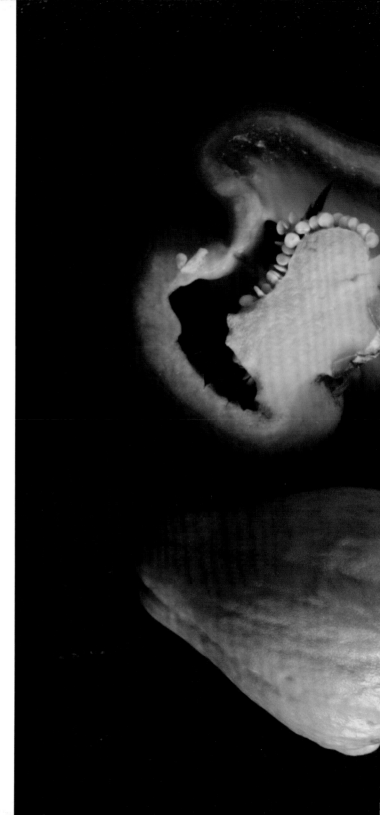

FOR OUR SISTERS
LYNN MALTZ, ROBIN BLUT, PATTY FOX, JACKIE
HARDEE, SANDY GAIL MORE & BRIDGET MORE

CONTENTS

FOREWORD

New Orleans' obsession with food is hardly a secret. At breakfast, the primary topic of conversation is what we will have for lunch. At lunch, we talk about dinner. And so on.

This is a cherished local custom that crosses all social, political, racial, and economic boundaries.

The primary exception to this forward-looking cultural tradition is the backward-looking obsession with where all this food came from, what are the ingredients, who made it, and where did the recipe come from?

That last question lingers in the collective psyche; south Louisianans are fiercely proud and protective of their family recipes. Everyone thinks they make something the best, and many claim to have made it first.

The number of men who claim to have invented turducken could fill the main dining room of Antoine's restaurant, which, by the way, lays claim to the creation of Oysters Rockefeller. And so on again.

But many of the region's most popular dishes are of unknowable provenance. Did anyone actually create, say, gumbo or jambalaya, or shrimp bisque?

Well, maybe, in the same way that someone "created" jazz or blues or rock and roll; we just don't know who that exact "somebody" is.

These cultural treasures were not born of a specific moment in the space-time continuum, but are the products of many hands and minds — legions of ideas, innovations, and techniques developed over centuries, passed around, imprinted by various nationalities, and ethnicities, influenced by neighboring cultures and tribes, adopted, adapted, and rearranged by immigrants and interlopers alike.

And somewhere along the way, a specific recipe is codified, embraced, institutionalized. It becomes official: THIS is how you make Pot au Feu or Chicken Bonne Femme.

These are the kinds of recipes that are prepared, preserved, and nurtured by the keepers of tradition and culture. They have outlived and outlasted lesser variants of their day.

The recipes in this book all fall under the classification of Creole cooking. We don't claim that these are the only ways to make these dishes; rather, these are the best ways — simple, classical, traditional, and time-tested.

But before you can understand what best constitutes the creation of a Creole dish, there is another more vexing and complicated matter to resolve: What, exactly, is Creole? It's a common question in south Louisiana, with an uncommon answer. Often, it depends who you ask. Or who you are. Or what you believe.

Like turducken, the origins and history of many cultural traditions and icons are widely debated and disputed among adherents, practitioners, academics, folklorists, and the many venerated neighborhood griots, and keepers of the flame.

Jazz. Voodoo. The Mardi Gras Indians. What, exactly, are these things? How, exactly, did they begin? When and where were they created?

There are volumes of scholarly research on the origins of such things, but you'd be hard pressed to find universally accepted definitions of these cultural treasures, particularly in the way they exist in Louisiana today.

So, too, with the term "Creole."

This book uses Creole as an adjective to denote a specific genre of regional cooking birthed over the past two centuries from the country's most fertile and abundant fields, forests, and waterways

What this book is not, is a story of Creole people. That's a whole 'nuther story altogether, a whole 'nuther book.

WHAT OR WHO IS CREOLE?

The term "Creole" has a different meaning when applied to food as opposed to ethnicity. Yes, Creole cuisine comes from Creole people — just like Italian food comes from Italians and Vietnamese food comes from the Vietnamese.

But who are the Creoles? What is the meaning of the word? Well, like we said before … it's complicated.

The word Creole, as an adjective, is defined as any product or tradition born of the mixing of French, Spanish, and African cultures in the New World. Hence, Creole cuisine.

But the definition of a Creole person is more elusive, more complicated, often mistaken. It is commonly tossed about casually in New Orleans, a blanket term to describe light-skinned African-Americans. This misses the mark by a wide margin.

Generally Creole is defined as a person born of European parents in America, specifically in French or Spanish colonies, particularly in and around Louisiana. They are first-generation immigrants.

The confusion comes from the second definition that dictionaries offer for the term to describe the dark-skinned descendants of the indigenous population of the West Indies, particularly Haiti, as opposed to Africans imported during times of slavery.

Two hundred years ago, the largest populations of both Creole populations in the New World merged in New Orleans, eventually intermingling and helping create the rich ethnic diversity that characterizes the city's current population. In general, Creoles were residents of New Orleans and Cajuns were from southwest Louisiana.

Creole cooking has been influenced over the years by the Cajuns of southwestern Louisiana, the massive African population—both freed and enslaved, by the Native Americans who were here first, and later from waves of Haitian, German, Italian, English and Irish immigrants.

THE PETTICOAT REBELLION.

Creole cooking comprises a veritable gumbo of cultures, nationalities and techniques, brought to bear upon the diverse and flavorful harvests, and bounties of the region's fertile soils, lush forests, and abundant waters.

In the early 18th century, France dispatched its first shipload of women to its Gulf Coast settlements to provide wives for the male inhabitants, and ensure population growth in its valued territories.

Domestic bliss was short-lived, however, as the women quickly grew tired of the constant shortages of wheat, flour, vegetables, and herbs, forced to build their dietary regimens on the local corn.

By 1722, they'd had enough. Marching on the Governor's residence in New Orleans, the women banged on pots and pans, demanding an audience —and more and better food. Hence was born the Petticoat Rebellion.

Governor Jean Baptiste Le Moyne was quick to find a solution. His housekeeper, a Madame Langois, was widely regarded as the colony's finest cook. Le Moyne directed her to introduce them to the vast local resources and the techniques to bring out their finest flavors — file powder for what would become gumbo; ground meal to make hominy grits. And so on.

Thus was established America's first cooking school. An anxious population was placated. And Creole cooking was born.

Yes, it's a little more complicated than that, but historians do generally mark the Petticoat Rebellion as the seminal moment that established and disseminated a particular style of cooking that we now hail as the country's most important contribution to the dining canon. It has changed often, evolved, matured, and blossomed over time.

It started evolving with first ships that docked in the vibrant port city and evolves today in the kitchens of celebrity chefs who continue to experiment, blend, fuse, and expand the notion of Creole cooking.

- Chris Rose

MEATS, POULTRY *and* SEAFOOD

Like most aspects of Creole cuisine, the meat used in New Orleans' cooking is a considerable mix of what the European settlers were familiar with and what they found in the New World.

The original French explorers came with limited supplies aboard the small ships that brought them across the Atlantic. Subsequent voyages brought more supplies, both animals and plants, as well as the equipment to be used in their production.

While the first French settlers had cattle and pigs, they were more interested in breeding their stock than eating them. They did this quite efficiently. At the beginning of the 17th century there were less than 20 cattle in Louisiana, by 1746 there were an estimated 10,000 head.

German immigrants in the area, like other ethnic groups, formed their own community. Germantown was just upriver of New Orleans, and specialized in pig farming. This local abundance of pigs left a lasting effect on Creole cooking, in the abundance of pork products utilized in many dishes.

While cattle in Louisiana were supplemented by animals brought in from the already established settlements in the Caribbean, the Creoles also had ready access to native game.

Native Americans taught the new settlers how to survive in the unfamiliar, seemingly hostile area. From using sassafras to grinding cornmeal, hunting in the swamps, and fishing the bayous, the newcomers modified their familiar recipes and created new one from the bounty.

The cooks of New Orleans were exposed to both the salt water fish of the Gulf such as the pompano, as well as the fresh water fishes of the inland waterways. The native shellfish also became a centerpiece for Creole cuisine, from clams and oysters to crawfish, shrimp, and crabs.

While the European settlers brought chickens and other fowl with them, they also found plentiful birds in the area including turkey and quail, which were all incorporated into their culinary culture.

Tujague's Restaurant
BEEF BRISKET

For fix-it-and-forget-it ease, after the initial browning of the brisket it can be finished off in a slow cooker set to low for at least 8 hours, or until the brisket is fork-tender. In a hurry? Use a pressure cooker according to the manufacturer's specifications. In either case, remove the meat when it is cooked and thicken the sauce as directed below.

SERVES 12 to 16

2 tablespoons vegetable oil
a 5-pound beef brisket
2 large onions, chopped
4 cloves garlic, chopped
2 large carrots, chopped
2 cups chopped tomatoes
2 stalks celery, chopped
1 tablespoon chili powder
3 bay leaves
1 tablespoon chopped curly parsley
1 tablespoon fresh thyme, chopped
1 teaspoon allspice
1 teaspoon whole black peppercorns
1 teaspoon liquid smoke flavoring
1 tablespoon balsamic vinegar
beef stock to cover

1. In a heavy pot or Dutch oven heat the oil over high heat, in it brown the brisket on both sides, and transfer the brisket to a plate.

2. Add the onion, garlic, and carrot to the pot and sauté, stirring, until browned. Return the brisket to the pot and add the tomatoes, celery, chili powder, bay leaves, parsley, thyme, allspice, peppercorns, liquid smoke, and balsamic vinegar. Add enough beef stock to cover the brisket and simmer, covered, for 3 hours. The brisket should be fork-tender but not falling apart. Remove the brisket and cut it into 1/4-inch slices or large chucks.

3. Increase the heat slightly to reduce the stock. When the stock has reduced by half, strain out any solids, discarding them, return the stock to the pot with the brisket, and heat through. Serve warm.

Legendary Tujague's is the second-longest operating restaurant in New Orleans, dating from 1849. Over time, lunch at Tujague's came to mean a marvelous seven-course, liquor-fueled affair. In the early days, boiled beef brisket was one of only two entrées offered for lunch.

Tujague's Restaurant opened in 1856 and moved to Madame Begue's premises when she closed, so two of the first three restaurants in the city were at the same location, which can be a little confusing. What is clear, however, is that Tujague's still serves a fine example of the classic Creole meal of boiled beef.

Leftovers make magnificent roast beef po-boys — good enough to simply cook a brisket just for that pleasure. An added bonus is the liquid left behind, to strain and reserve, frozen, for later use as aromatic beef stock.

RED *and* WHITE HORSERADISH SAUCES

RED HORSERADISH SAUCE
1 cup ketchup
5 tablespoons prepared horseradish
1 tablespoon salt
1 tablespoon freshly ground black pepper

Mix all ingredients together in a small bowl and refrigerate, covered, for at least 1 hour prior to serving.

WHITE HORSERADISH SAUCE
2 cups heavy cream
5 tablespoons prepared horseradish
1 tablespoon salt
1 teaspoon cracked black pepper

In a large bowl beat the cream until it forms stiff peaks. Fold in the horseradish, salt, and pepper and refrigerate, covered, for at least 1 hour prior to serving.

Chef John Folse's rendition of this Creole classic differs little from one for Daube d'Italienne, published in 1907 in The New York Times and attributed to Madame Begué, save for her call to serve the Daube over macaroni with a "good grating of Italian cheese."

Daube is still regularly glorified at the Christmas table as Daube Glacée, which involves the addition of gelatin and served cold on toast points. It usually made an appearance as an entrée in the Creoles' Réveillon feast following midnight Mass on Christmas Eve.

Cold and gelatinous or not — we prefer warm — the humble dish can be swanked up by substituting veal eye-of-the-round roast or short ribs for the less expensive beef shoulder, rump, round, or chuck roast traditionally called for.

When we first prepared this recipe, the "Ah ha" moment was adding tomato sauce — Italian pot roast on fettuccine, albeit somewhat heartier, and richer than a standard pot roast recipe.

In the unlikely event that leftovers are available, they make superb beef debris po-boys.

Chef Folse and fellow chef Rick Tramonto, together opened Restaurant R'evolution at the Royal Sonesta Hotel. The French Quarter establishment is Folse's entry into New Orleans as a contemporary Creole extravaganza. They call it a modern, imaginative reinterpretation of classic Cajun and Creole cuisine. We call it just plain good eating.

He's written several cookbooks, the most recent being "After the Hunt: Louisiana's Authoritative Collection of Wild Game & Game Fish Cookery." An earlier work, "The Encyclopedia of Cajun and Creole Cuisine," is a labor of love about the state's culinary history.

There's not much Folse doesn't do for Louisiana's culinary community. For example, he was the driving force behind the establishment of the John Folse Culinary Institute at Nicholls State University.

Chef John Folse, R'evolution
BEEF DAUBE

Modern recipes often call for browning the beef in olive oil as opposed to larding with pork fat. It is most often made with a tough, inexpensive cut of meat, rendered fork-tender through slow braising. Combining French braising technique with an Italian red gravy, Beef Daube embodies the turn-of-the-20th-century marriage between the Sicilian immigrants who poured into New Orleans beginning in 1880 and the settled Italian immigrants who had already established a foothold, dating back to the French era.

SERVES 4 to 6

1/4 pound salt pork fat
one 5-pound beef shoulder roast
1/4 cup salt
1/4 cup freshly ground black pepper
1/2 cup minced garlic
1/2 cup bacon drippings or vegetable oil
2 cups diced onions
2 cups diced celery
1 cup diced bell peppers
1/4 cup tomato sauce
2 cups diced carrots
1 cup dry red wine
1 quart beef stock
fettuccine, cooked for serving

1. Cut the salt pork fat into 1/4-inch-wide strips about 2-inches long. Using a sharp knife, cut 6 to 8 slits into the shoulder roast. Stuff the slits with the salt pork fat, half the salt, half the pepper, and half the garlic, and season the roast on all sides with the remaining salt and pepper.

2. In a cast-iron Dutch oven melt the bacon drippings or oil over medium-high heat and brown the roast on all sides. When the roast is evenly browned, add the onion, celery, bell peppers, and remaining garlic and sauté for 3 to 5 minutes, or until the vegetables are wilted. Stir in the tomato sauce, carrots, and red wine. Pour in the beef stock, bring to a rolling boil, and reduce the heat to a simmer.

3. Cook the beef, covered, for 2 1/2 hours, or until it is tender, and season to taste.

4. Toss warm fettuccine in sauce and serve with the beef.

Chef John Besh, Lüke
GRILLADES *and* GRITS

Though Chef John Besh's version of this braised dish is traditionally served for a leisurely weekend breakfast or brunch, it's also welcome here for lunch or dinner. It calls for pricey veal shoulder, but thin medallions of round steak or sliced pork tenderloin work as well without giving up flavor.

SERVES 6 to 8

4 pounds boneless veal shoulder, sliced into thin cutlets
salt and freshly ground black pepper
2 cups all-purpose flour
2 teaspoons Creole seasoning (*see page 67*)
1/4 cup rendered bacon fat
1 large onion, diced
1 stalk celery, diced
1/2 red bell pepper, diced
2 cloves garlic, minced
2 cups canned whole plum tomatoes, drained, seeded, and diced
2 cups veal stock
leaves from 1 sprig of fresh thyme
1 teaspoon crushed red pepper flakes
1 bay leaf
1 tablespoon Worcestershire sauce
Tabasco sauce to taste
2 scallions, chopped

1. Season the veal cutlets with salt and pepper. In a large shallow bowl combine the flour and Creole spice mix. Dredge the cutlets in the flour mixture, shake off any excess, and reserve a tablespoon of the seasoned flour. In a large skillet over high heat, heat the bacon fat and in it fry the cutlets, in batches so as not to crowd the skillet, until golden brown on both sides, and set them aside.

2. Reduce the heat to medium-high, add the onion, and cook, stirring constantly, until it reaches a deep mahogany. Add the celery, bell pepper, and garlic, and continue cooking until the vegetables are tender, about 5 minutes. Stir in the reserved tablespoon of seasoned flour.

3. Increase the heat to high and stir in the tomatoes and veal stock. Bring the liquid to a boil, reduce the heat to medium, and stir in the thyme, pepper flakes, bay leaf, and Worcestershire sauce. Return the cutlets to the skillet, reduce the heat to a simmer, and cook, covered, until the veal is fork-tender, about 45 minutes. Season to taste with salt, black pepper, and the Tabasco sauce and fold in the chopped scallions. Serve immediately over Jalapeño Cheese Grits.

Both Creole and Cajun cooks lay claim to the origins of grillades. No matter, the practice of first searing in hot fat then slowly braising an inexpensive cut of meat in a roux-based gravy is inherent to both culinary genres. Through the slow-cooking process, aromatic vegetables and meat break down into a hearty meat-laced gravy.

JALAPEÑO CHEESE GRITS

These cheesy grits are perfect with almost anything.

SERVES 6–8

1 cup stone-ground white corn grits
1 jalapeño pepper
3 tablespoons butter
2 tablespoons mascarpone or cream cheese
1/4 cup grated Edam cheese

1. Heat 4 cups of water in a large heavy-bottomed pot over high heat until it comes to a boil. Slowly pour in the grits, whisking constantly. Reduce the heat to low, and cook, covered, stirring occasionally with a wooden spoon, for about 20 minutes.

2. While the grits are cooking, pan-roast the jalapeño pepper in a small skillet over high heat until the skin is brown and blistered. Cut the pepper in half lengthwise and remove the skin and the seeds, discarding them. Mince the flesh and add it to the pot of grits.

3. Remove the pot from the heat and fold in the butter, mascarpone, and Edam cheese. Season with salt to taste.

As production commando and chief test cook, Barry made this recipe so many times it became even more famous.

He also got jealous about his stock and reduced the remaining liquid, then strained it into small jars of intense flavor to enhance future recipes. No one told him that the French have been doing that for centuries, with exactly the same dish, for that exact reason: flavor.

Pot au feu may be cooled then covered and refrigerated. Any remaining fat will solidify, floating to the top, to be removed, if desired.

Horseradish sauce is a tangy accompaniment, recipes are on page 15.

Barry Garner
POT *au* FEU

Pot au feu, pot on the fire, is a classic French recipe for beef stew, happily translated and embraced by New Orleanians. It generally contains an inexpensive cut of beef to be cooked for a long time, any variety of aromatic vegetables, and seasonings.

SERVES 6

1/4 cup olive oil
six 8-ounce bone-in short ribs
1 leek, white part only, washed thoroughly and chopped
2 large carrots, peeled and chopped
3 stalks celery, chopped
36 pearl onions, peeled
salt and freshly ground black pepper to taste
1/2 cup all-purpose flour
2 cups red wine
18 fingerling potatoes, halved
3 quarts beef stock
4 sprigs of fresh thyme
2 bay leaves
1/4 cup balsamic vinegar
scallions for garnish
French bread to serve, warmed

1. In a Dutch oven over high heat, heat the olive oil and in it brown the short ribs, in batches if necessary, on all sides. Transfer the ribs to a plate and set aside.

2. Add the leek, carrot, celery, and pearl onions, season with the salt and pepper, and sauté until tender. Stir in the flour, being careful not to let clumps form, add the wine, and continue to cook for about 15 minutes, or until the mixture is reduced by half.

3. Return the ribs to the Dutch oven and add the fingerling potatoes, beef stock, thyme, and bay leaves. Reduce the heat to a simmer and cook, stirring frequently, for 4 hours.

4. Remove the thyme stems and the bay leaves, add the balsamic vinegar, and serve immediately, garnished with the spring onions and accompanied by the French bread.

Chef Chris Lynch, Café Atchafalaya
CANE-GLAZED QUAIL

Quail roasted quickly at a high heat then simply brushed with a cane glaze creates a delicately flavored Louisiana favorite.

SERVES 4

For the Cane Glaze
1 shallot, cut into very thin strips
3 cloves garlic, roughly chopped
8 sprigs of thyme
1/2 bunch parsley stems
2 cups Steen's Cane Syrup
2 tablespoons Worcestershire sauce
2 tablespoons Crystal Hot Sauce

For the Quail
4 small quails, cleaned
salt and freshly ground black pepper to taste
1 cup Dirty Rice

Prepare the Cane Glaze

1. Combine all the ingredients in a small saucepan and simmer over medium heat for 20 to 30 minutes, or until reduced to 1/3 the volume.

2. Strain out the solids and use the glaze immediately or store in an airtight container in the refrigerator.

Prepare the Quail

1. Preheat the oven to 400 degrees and turn the grill on to high heat.

2. Season the quail very lightly inside and out with salt and pepper and place on the grill for one minute. Give the quail a quarter turn and grill for another minute to create a cross-hatch pattern. Turn the quails over and repeat on the other side.

3. Stuff each cavity with the dirty rice mixture.

4. Transfer the quails to a roasting pan, brush thoroughly with the Cane Glaze, and roast for 5 to 6 minutes, or until they are golden brown.

DIRTY RICE

SERVES 4

2 chicken livers, minced
1/8 pound ground sirloin
1/4 yellow onion, diced
1/2 green bell pepper, diced
1 1/2 celery stalks, diced
2 cloves garlic, finely diced
2 thyme sprigs, leaves only
2 tablespoons chopped parsley
1 tablespoon paprika
1 teaspoon cayenne
1/2 quart chicken stock
1 cup uncooked white rice

1. In a large saucepan over medium heat sauté the chicken livers and sirloin for 3 to 5 minutes, or until some of their fat has rendered off. Add the onion, bell pepper, celery, and garlic and cook for 8 to 10 minutes, or until the vegetables have browned lightly. Fold in the thyme leaves, parsley, paprika, and cayenne.

2. Add the chicken stock to the pan and bring to a boil. Stir in the rice and return to a boil. Reduce the heat to a simmer and cook, covered, for 30 minutes. If the rice becomes dry, add more chicken stock. Reserve 1 cup to stuff the quail.

Serve the remaining dirty rice as a side or mound around the quail.

In 1880, Emile Commander founded what would ultimately become one of the city's most famous establishments, following a series of ups, downs, and natural disasters occurring over a century in business.

New Orleans' most gracious culinary matriarch, Ella Brennan, first made her mark at the Brennan's of Royal Street establishment, prior to the rambling family's division of restaurants, which resulted in her side of the family embracing Commander's Palace.

Ella, her sisters Dottie and Adelaide, along with their brother Dick revitalized Commander's Palace. The siblings introduced their children to the business, sprouting even more restaurants across the city.

Ti Adelaide Martin and Lally Brennan are this generation's co-proprietors. They have beautifully renovated and invigorated Commander's Palace from top to bottom, from kitchens to dining rooms. They created Cafe Adelaide and SoBou, while authoring several cookbooks.

Probably the most respected legend in our restaurant world, Ella set high standards that are still followed today.

Paul Prudhomme, Emeril Lagasse, and the late Jamie Shannon were executive chefs under her reign. They have each contributed to a grand, enviable legacy.

In the Garden District, surrounded by oak trees and sprawling onto a leafy courtyard, Commander's Palace continues to flourish.

Chef Tory McPhail, Commander's Palace
SOFT SHELL CRAB

Blue crabs molt, losing their hard shells. We happily anticipate this seasonal wardrobe change, dreaming of crunchy fried soft shells elegantly served as Tory McPhail dresses them, or simply between French bread on po-boy sandwiches

SERVES 4

4 large soft shell crabs, cleaned
1 cup all-purpose flour
1 cup breadcrumbs
3 large eggs
3/4 cup milk
1/2 cup Remoulade Sauce (see page 39)
1 teaspoon lemon juice
1/4 cup sliced heart of palm
2 Creole tomatoes, diced
1/4 cup fresh Italian parsley leaves, chopped
1/2 cup mixed greens
salt and freshly ground black pepper to taste
vegetable oil for cooking

1. Ask your seafood seller to clean the crabs, or easily do it yourself; Holding the crab in one hand, with a pair of kitchen scissors cut off the face (eyes and mouth). Cut off the little flap at the crab bottom, pull top shell sides up, and cut off gills. Puncture the water sack behind the eyes and squeeze to remove water.

2. Heat enough oil to measure 4 inches deep in a tall, wide heavy pot to 375 degrees. In a large, shallow dish combine the flour and breadcrumbs. Mix well and set aside. In a small bowl whisk together the eggs with the milk to form an egg wash.

3. Place the remaining 2 cups flour in a shallow bowl. Dredge each crab in the flour mixture, being sure to coat the legs. Dip the dredged crab in the egg wash, letting the excess batter drip off. Dredge again in the flour mixture and shake off the excess.

4. Gently slide 2 crabs in the hot oil, belly side up. Place a ladle on the belly of each crab to keep it on the bottom, resting ladle handle against the side of the pan. Fry the crabs until golden brown, about 4 minutes, making sure oil returns to 375 degrees before adding more crabs. Drain the crabs on paper towels.

5. In a small bowl, toss the 1/4 cup Remoulade Sauce and the lemon juice with the heart of palm, diced tomatoes, parsley, and mixed greens. Sauce four plates with the remaining Remoulade Sauce and place a crab on each plate. Add equal amounts of the vegetable medley to the center of each crab and serve immediately.

Chef Michael Regua Sr., Antoine's

CRABMEAT *au* GRATIN

The recipe is simple. The result is stunning. The secret is jumbo lump crabmeat, as fresh as the morning harvest. There are no shortcuts, or substitutions. None are needed.

SERVES 6

1 1/4 cups Béchamel sauce
2 1/2 cups lump crabmeat (preferably Louisiana blue crab)
salt and freshly ground black pepper to taste
4 tablespoons grated Cheddar cheese
4 tablespoons grated Romano cheese
4 tablespoons grated Mozzarella cheese
1/4 cup breadcrumbs

1. Preheat the oven to 400 degrees.

2. In a medium saucepan, gently fold the béchamel sauce and crabmeat together using a rubber spatula. Be careful not to break up the crabmeat. Season with salt and pepper, and cook over medium heat for 1 to 2 minutes. Divide equally among 6 oven-safe ramekins or small dishes.

3. In a small bowl, mix all the cheeses with the breadcrumbs and divide equally among the ramekins.

4. Bake for 12 to 15 minutes, or until the tops begin to brown. Let cool for 5 to 10 minutes and serve warm.

When she visits New Orleans, a dear friend refuses to depart the city without having more than her fair share of Antoine's Crabmeat au Gratin.

Antoine's is the country's oldest family owned and operated restaurant, established in 1840, and still a New Orleans tradition.

BÉCHAMEL SAUCE

MAKES 1 1/4 cups

3 tablespoons unsalted butter
3 tablespoons all-purpose flour
1 cup whole milk
1/4 cup thinly sliced white onion
1 whole clove
1 bay leaf
salt and freshly ground white pepper to taste

1. In a saucepan over low heat melt the butter. Add the flour, a teaspoon at a time and cook for about 2 minutes, stirring constantly, to form a paste. Remove the roux from the heat and set aside. *(see page 88)*

2. In a separate saucepan over medium-high heat, combine the milk, onion, clove, and bay leaf. Bring to a boil, reduce heat to medium-low, and cook 4 to 5 minutes.

3. Reduce heat and whisk the roux into the milk mixture until it has been completely combined. Allow to simmer for about 2 minutes, or until the sauce will stick to the back of a spoon. Whisk in salt and pepper to taste.

4. Strain the sauce through a fine colander to remove the onion, clove, and bay leaf. Use immediately.

Like the city's native Creole cuisine, the fine dining standards of these historic establishments came by way of evolution.

Galatoire's has been serving for well over a century, established by Jean Galatoire in 1905.

New Orleans enjoys distinction as one of the world's great culinary capitols. As such, the city is celebrated for its many restaurants, a collection of which were established in the mid 19th century and remain in operation.

New Orleans first eateries—including Antoine's—aspired to do little more than provide mere sustenance and were classified as "restaurants" simply because they "served food to the public." Many were simply a boarding house that served meals. At the time there wasn't any need for an upscale restaurant.

The Civil War was in the future, and domestic slaves made dining and entertaining at home easy and convenient for the owners, so that's what the wealthy upper class did. Only the working class took meals outside of the home: Working stiffs had to get food in them to keep on working .

It was the late 1800s and early 1900s, before ladies of good family even considered dining in public establishments such as restaurants.

Chef Michael Sichel, Galatoire's
CRABMEAT MAISON

Only the finest quality jumbo lump Gulf crab (please avoid using pasteurized crabmeat if at all possible) should be used for this elegant dish, which, while perfect as a salad or cold appetizer also makes for a lovely luncheon entrée.

SERVES 6

2 egg yolks
2 tablespoons red-wine vinegar
1 tablespoon Creole mustard or any coarse, grainy brown mustard
1 teaspoon lemon juice
1 cup vegetable oil
4 tablespoons capers, drained
4 tablespoons chopped scallions (green and white parts)
1 tablespoon chopped fresh parsley
white pepper and salt to taste
1 pound jumbo lump crabmeat, cleaned
1 small head iceberg lettuce, cut into thin ribbons, washed, drained, and dried
2 medium tomatoes, preferably Creole, cored and cut into 3-inch-thick slices

1. Combine the egg yolks, vinegar, Creole mustard, and lemon juice in a food processor and process for two minutes. With the processor running, add the oil slowly in a thin stream and process until emulsified.

2. Transfer to a mixing bowl and gently fold in the capers, scallions, and parsley. Add the white pepper and salt to taste and chill for 2 to 4 hours.

3. Just before serving, gently fold in the crabmeat, taking care not to break up the lumps.

4. Divide the lettuce among 6 plates, top with a tomato slice, and spoon the crab over the tomato.

Chef Michelle McRaney, Mr. B's Bistro
JUMBO LUMP CRAB CAKES

Justifiably famous for them, Mr. B's does crab cakes right — with knuckle-sized lumps of crabmeat bound together in a light mixture that includes Panko breadcrumbs, which lend a pleasant crunch against the silky crab. Use unpasteurized Gulf crabmeat if at all possible and, when folding the mixture, take care not to break up the delicate lumps. Chef Michelle McRaney's addition of half a finely minced Anaheim chile pepper to her Ravigote Sauce lends a bite that cuts through the richness of the dish.

SERVES 8 as an appetizer or 4 as an entrée

1/2 medium red bell pepper, diced
1/2 medium green bell pepper, diced
1/3 cup mayonnaise
1/4 cup Panko
3 scallions, thinly sliced
juice of 1/4 lemon
1/4 teaspoon Crystal hot sauce
1/4 teaspoon Creole seasoning
1/2 cup all-purpose flour
1/2 teaspoon salt
1/4 teaspoon freshly ground black pepper
1 pound jumbo lump crabmeat
2 tablespoons unsalted butter
Ravigote Sauce as an accompaniment

1. In a large mixing bowl combine the bell peppers, mayonnaise, Panko, scallions, lemon juice, hot sauce, Creole seasoning, flour, and the salt and pepper to taste. Fold in the crabmeat, being careful not to break up any lumps.

2. Form crab cakes using a 2 1/2-inch-across cookie cutter, filling the cutter about I inch thick with crabmeat. Place the crab cakes on a baking sheet and chill for I hour.

3. In a large skillet melt the butter over medium heat and in it cook the crab cakes until lightly browned on both sides, flipping once. Serve immediately accompanied by the Ravigote Sauce.

So cherished are Louisiana blue crabs that 70 percent of what is served up at East Coast crab boils as Maryland crabs are actually Grade A male Louisiana blue crabs. Found abundantly in the bayous, rivers, and inlets of Louisiana and harvested year-round, with a summertime peak, our crabs are revered for their delicate sweet flavor and cooking versatility.

Mr. B's stands for Brennan's, another mighty offshoot of the restaurant group—the Commander's Palace side of the family. Managing Partner Cindy Brennan works closely with Executive Chef Michelle McRaney to provide Creole-style specialties in the French Quarter.

RAVIGOTE SAUCE

MAKES 1 1/2 cups

2 1/2 teaspoons fresh lemon juice
1/2 teaspoon dry mustard
1 1/4 cups mayonnaise
1/2 red bell pepper, finely diced
1/2 large Anaheim chile pepper, finely diced
1 hard-boiled egg, diced
1 tablespoon finely chopped flat-leaf parsley
2 3/4 teaspoons prepared horseradish
1 1/4 teaspoons Dijon mustard
3/4 teaspoon dried tarragon

In a medium bowl combine all the ingredients and mix together well. Serve, chilled, immediately or store in an airtight container in the refrigerator until ready to use.

In New Orleans, Leah Chase holds the undisputed title of Queen of Creole Cuisine. Her realm is headquartered at Dooky Chase's, her family restaurant.

Before desegregation, it was a place for people of color. Today, race, creed or zip code doesn't matter a whit at Dooky Chase's. Leah and her husband, Dooky, created one of the country's most culturally significant restaurants, grown from a sandwich shop.

She has welcomed and cooked for such luminaries as the Rev. Martin Luther King, Jr., Duke Ellington, Thurgood Marshall, James Baldwin, and Ray Charles, who regularly stopped by for her gumbo, jambalaya, fried chicken, red beans and rice, plus a long list of other Creole classics.

She also has hosted several presidents of the United States in the dining rooms, where she displays prints and paintings by some of America's most respected artists, including a good many New Orleanians.

Her smile and gracious manner let you know immediately that she's a lady — a lady to be reckoned with. Her charitable, civic and professional efforts have been repeatedly recognized, although she seeks nothing but to feed her guests properly and serve her community.

Following Hurricane Katrina, the restaurant faced a tough two-year comeback. Leah and Dooky have given so much that asking for help never occurred to them. Bit by bit they started rebuilding and refurbishing. It was time for others to return the favor. Spontaneous support, gifts and contributions — large and small — arrived from friends, restaurateurs, patrons, and colleagues.

Leah says that one should strive to make a person feel his or her worth, that this is a true measure of a person. "I had to get back on my feet," she told me, "so I can start giving back."

Now in her 90s, she's still cooking, still giving back.

Chef Leah Chase, Dooky Chase's
CRABMEAT and SHRIMP FARCI

This savory combination of shrimp, crabmeat, and seasonings creates a local favorite.

A friend's child once argued that "little kids shouldn't have to eat purple food," in hopes of avoiding eggplant. Peeled, prepared, and served in a casserole dish, there's nary a purple shade to be seen. Leah's Crabmeat Farci and Shrimp is reason enough to simply stand in front of the chaffing dish, effectively blocking any other enthusiasts.

SERVES 4

2 medium eggplants
1/4 pound butter
1 pound shrimp (peeled, deveined, and chopped)
1 cup chopped onion
1 tablespoon chopped garlic
1 tablespoon chopped parsley
1 tablespoon salt
1/2 teaspoon cayenne pepper
1/2 pound white crabmeat, well picked-over
1/2 teaspoon whole thyme leaves
1 1/2 cups seasoned breadcrumbs

1. Cut eggplants in half. With a tablespoon, scoop out the insides carefully, leaving about 1/4-inch shells. Cut the removed insides into small cubes. Soak the shells and cubes in separate pans of water for 15 to 30 minutes to draw out any bitterness. Let shells and cubes drain well on paper towels.

2. In a heavy saucepan melt the butter and add the cubed eggplant, shrimp, and onion. Cover and cook over medium heat for 40 minutes. Add the garlic, parsley, salt, and cayenne, stirring well, and cook, uncovered, long enough to reduce as much of the liquid as possible. (Shrimp and eggplants give off quite a bit of juice.)

3. Preheat oven to 350 degrees. Stir in the crabmeat and cook for 10 minutes more. Remove from heat and add the thyme leaves and breadcrumbs, stirring until mixed in well. Stuff the well-drained shells with the eggplant mixture. Place in baking pan and sprinkle with more breadcrumbs. Dot the tops with butter and bake for 20 minutes.

JoAnn Clevenger, Upperline
FRIED GREEN TOMATOES
with SHRIMP REMOULADE

Fried green tomatoes is a Southern/Creole dish elevated to a whole new taste by the addition of Shrimp Remoulade. The two classic recipes were first combined in Upperline's kitchen.

SERVES 4

FOR THE REMOULADE SAUCE
1/2 cup Creole mustard
2 tablespoons ketchup
1 teaspoon Worcestershire sauce
2 teaspoons prepared horseradish
1 teaspoon garlic, finely chopped
1 teaspoon fresh lemon juice
1 1/2 teaspoons paprika
1/8 teaspoon ground white pepper
1/8 teaspoon cayenne pepper
salt to taste
1/2 cup olive oil
1/4 cup finely chopped heart of celery
1 1/2 teaspoons finely chopped parsley
1 tablespoon grated onion
1 tablespoon finely chopped scallion tops
Tabasco sauce to taste

FOR THE TOMATOES
5 tablespoons vegetable oil
1 cup buttermilk
1 cup corn flour, lightly seasoned with salt and black pepper
8 slices green tomato, 1/2-inch thick
2 cups mixed greens
24 medium shrimp, peeled and boiled

Prepare the Remoulade Sauce

1. Combine the Creole mustard, ketchup, Worcestershire, horseradish, garlic, lemon juice, paprika, white pepper, cayenne pepper, and salt in a small food processor. Turn the processor on to low speed and in a slow, steady stream, add the olive oil until completely incorporated.

2. Fold in the remaining ingredients and store, covered, in the refrigerator until chilled. If made in advance, the sauce can last several days if kept covered in the refrigerator.

The word "restaurant" was "to restore," says Upperline's proprietor JoAnn Clevenger. "Originally restaurants were more than just a place to find a meal; restaurants existed to soothe and bolster the weary soul with comfort and indulgence."

As the owner, she has made the Upperline her home, where she soothes her guests.

Although the dish is common in New Orleans today, the original fried green tomato with the shrimp rémoulade combination was created at the Upperline in 1992 by Chef Tom Cowman.

Chef Tom made the Upperline his last restaurant. Artist Rise Ochsner immortalized him in a magnificent portrait, which hangs in the art-filled front dining room. It is a grand and quirky collection, not unlike the combination of classic and contemporary cuisine that is modern New Orleans.

Prepare the Tomatoes

1. In a large sauté pan, heat the oil over medium heat. Place the buttermilk and milk flour in separate shallow dishes. Once the oil is heated, dip the tomato slices in the buttermilk, then the corn flour, to coat both sides.

2. Carefully place the slices in the sauté pan and cook until the bottom is golden brown, then flip and finish cooking until the other side is golden brown as well.

On each of 4 serving plates, place 1/2 cup mixed greens and place two warm tomato slices on each bed of greens. Place 3 shrimp on each slice of tomato and drizzle about 2 tablespoons of Remoulade sauce over each plate.

Though increasingly associated with Creole cooking, the grits served with a stew or sauté of shrimp simply isn't so. The dish, "Shrimp Grits" or "Breakfast Shrimp" started out as a seasonal fisherman's dish of shrimp cooked in bacon grease served over creamy grits in the Low Country of the Carolinas. The simple seafood breakfast became an iconic Southern dish after Craig Claiborne wrote about it in The New York Times in 1985. We embraced it.

Chef John Besh is one of New Orleans heroes, celebrating our culinary heritage across the country by word of mouth. His foundation benefits a multitude of civic and charitable efforts.

(recipe continued from right)

Prepare the Shrimp

1. In a large saucepan over medium heat, heat the olive oil. While the olive oil is heating, season the shrimp with salt and Creole Seasoning. Add the shrimp to the pan and cook until they start to brown but are not cooked all the way through. Transfer the shrimp to a plate and set aside.

2. In the pan, sauté the andouille, garlic, shallot, peppers, and thyme until they become aromatic, about 5 minutes. Add the shrimp stock and bring to a simmer. Stir in the butter and reduce the sauce, stirring, for 3 to 5 minutes, or until it has thickened.

3. Return the shrimp to the pan and cook through, about 5 minutes. Add the lemon juice, diced tomatoes, and chives and heat through.

Spoon 1/2 cup of the grits into the middle of 6 bowls. Arrange 6 shrimp in the center, spoon the sauce around and over the shrimp and grits, and garnish with the chervil sprigs. Serve immediately.

Chef John Besh, Lüke
SHRIMP *and* GRITS

Chef John Besh enhances the flavor of an already hearty dish with the addition of minced andouille sausage. Cook the shrimp in batches and keep a close eye on them so they don't overcook. After sautéing on both sides, remove the shrimp from the skillet with tongs and return them to the pot once they're all cooked to the same doneness.

SERVES 6

FOR THE GRITS
1 teaspoon salt
1 cup white stone ground grits
2 tablespoons butter
1/2 cup mascarpone cheese

FOR THE SHRIMP
2 tablespoons olive oil
36 jumbo Louisiana shrimp
salt
Creole Seasoning (*see page 67*)
1/3 cup minced andouille sausage
2 cloves garlic, minced
1 shallot, minced
2 piquillo peppers, minced
1 tablespoon chopped thyme leaves
4 cups shrimp stock
2 tablespoons unsalted butter
1 teaspoon fresh lemon juice
2 cups canned diced tomatoes
1 tablespoon chopped fresh chives
1/2 cup fresh chervil sprigs

Prepare the Grits

1. In a medium-size heavy pot over high heat bring 4 cups of water to a boil and stir in the salt. Pour in the grits, stirring constantly, reduce the heat to low, and cook the grits, stirring occasionally, until all the water has been absorbed and the grits are soft, about 20 minutes. Add the butter and mascarpone, stirring until the cheese is melted, and remove the grit mixture from the heat. Place a sheet of plastic wrap directly on the surface of the grits to prevent a crust from forming.

(recipe continued at left)

Chef Wayne Bacquet, Li'l Dizzy's Café
SHRIMP CREOLE

Consider making the sauce the day before you plan to serve the dish. This will allow the flavors to marry and intensify, creating a strong counterpoint for the delicate flavor of the shrimp, which should be added after the sauce has been returned to a simmer.

SERVES 4

1 cup vegetable oil
3/4 cup all-purpose flour
1 1/2 medium onions, finely chopped
5 whole cloves garlic, peeled
2 bunches of scallions: green parts finely chopped; white parts roughly chopped
1/2 large green bell pepper, chopped
18 ounces tomato sauce
1 teaspoon fresh thyme, chopped
3 fresh bay leaves, crushed
1/4 teaspoon chopped fresh oregano
juice of 1/2 large lemon
2 1/2 cups water
1/4 teaspoon cayenne pepper
salt to taste
2 1/2 pounds shrimp, peeled and deveined
2 cups long-grain white rice, steamed or boiled

1. In a large, heavy-bottomed saucepan over medium-low heat, heat the oil, add the flour, stirring constantly and taking care no lumps form, until the roux turns the color of peanut butter. Reduce the heat and add the onion, garlic, scallion, and bell pepper. Stir well and cook for 4 to 6 minutes, or until the vegetables soften.

2. Stir in the tomato sauce, thyme, bay leaves, oregano, and lemon juice, return the heat to medium, and bring the sauce to a simmer. Stir in the water, cayenne, and salt to taste and simmer for 30 to 45 minutes, or until thickened.

3. Gently stir in the shrimp, reduce the heat to a bare simmer, and cook, covered, for 20 minutes. Allow to stand for 10 minutes and serve over the white rice.

It wouldn't be a Creole cookbook without Shrimp Creole, for goodness sake. At Li'l Dizzy's Café in the New Orleans Tremé neighborhood, Wayne Baquet carries on a Creole family restaurant tradition that began in 1947 when his grandfather opened Paul Gross Chicken Coop at the corner of Bienville and North Roman streets.

One of the first African-American owned restaurants in the city, Paul Gross Chicken Coop quickly established its reputation for fine, though affordable, Creole fare. Wayne's parents continued the tradition with Eddie's, their legendary Creole eatery in the city's 7th Ward that operated until the late 1990s.

When Wayne closed his own restaurant, Zachary's, here in the Carrollton area in 2004, he vowed to leave the restaurant business for good. But, fortunately, it's in his blood: He opened L'il Dizzy's in 2005 and we've all been happy ever since.

Hearty soul food was grafted to Creole cuisine in the Tremé neighborhood, combining two unique cooking styles whose roots have grown across the city and the country. It is our culinary DNA. Music for the mouth. Improvisation. A riff on the classics. Jazzy comfort food. Our psyche is deeply rooted in history, food, and music. Many revered New Orleans' chefs are also famous Tremé restaurateurs or have been fundamentally influenced by their heritage.

Tremé is thought to be the oldest African–American neighborhood in the country. Historically, it's the musical heart of the city, going all the way back to the 1700s, when slaves were allowed to gather in Congo Square (now contained within Louis Armstrong Park) to dance and play music.

Poppy Tooker loves to argue the virtues of red jambalaya versus brown jambalaya, which may well stimulate a cook-off to decide — with good eating all around. But there's hardly a gathering of any note that isn't celebrated with a potful of one or the other designed to make your soul and your taste buds sing. Author, broadcaster, and Southern food authority, Poppy began cooking with her grandmother and has never stopped.

POPPY'S TIPS:

~It is easiest to cook jambalaya in a cast-iron pot. The pot must be heavy enough to prevent burning and have a tightly fitting lid.

~Stock is always a better flavor alternative than water.

~Don't use breakfast or Italian sausage — their sage and fennel flavors have no place in jambalaya.

~Creole seasoning is all-purpose, so both Cajun and Creole cooks use it.

~To brown onions: Cook the onions in the oil over low heat until they are golden brown, stirring frequently. A little water helps prevent sticking.

~Turn your jambalaya only two or three times during cooking, scooping from the bottom to make sure the ingredients are evenly combined. Turn rather than stir, once the rice has been added, because this will prevent the jambalaya from getting mushy.

(recipe continued from right)

4. Remove the pot from the heat. Sprinkle the paprika over the jambalaya and, using a fork, gently fluff the scallions and paprika into the jambalaya.

5. Cover the jambalaya, let it stand for 10 minutes to let the flavors meld, and discard the bay leaf. Serve with the hot sauce, if you like.

Poppy Tooker
SHRIMP *and* HAM JAMBALAYA

Red is to city as brown is to country. New Orleans claims red, or Creole, and Cajun country claims brown. The fundamental difference is the addition of tomatoes in one of more of its guises, depending on the recipe. Seasoning is arbitrary, from spicy to mild — a matter of your own good taste.

SERVES 6 to 8

4 tablespoons unsalted butter
3 stalks celery, finely chopped
1 medium onion, finely chopped
1 green bell pepper, stemmed, seeded, and finely chopped
1/4 pound diced ham
1 pound peeled and deveined shrimp
3 tablespoons tomato paste
1 bay leaf
1/2 teaspoon chopped fresh thyme
1/4 teaspoon cayenne pepper
1/8 teaspoon chili powder
1/8 teaspoon ground allspice
a pinch ground cloves
1 1/2 teaspoons of Kosher salt
2 cups long-grain white rice
4 1/2 cups seafood stock
1 teaspoon sweet paprika
6 scallions, finely sliced
Louisiana hot sauce to taste, if desired

1. Melt the butter in a 5- to 6-quart enameled cast-iron Dutch oven (or other heavy-duty pot) over medium-high heat. Add the celery, onion, and bell pepper and cook, stirring often, about 7 minutes, or until softened.

2. Add the ham and the reserved shrimp and cook, stirring often, until any excess moisture evaporates and the ham and vegetables begin to brown, about 5 minutes. Add the tomato paste and cook, stirring, until the mixture is a shade darker, about 3 minutes. Stir in the bay leaf, thyme, cayenne, chili powder, allspice, cloves, and salt.

3. Fold in the rice very gently, add the reserved stock, and bring to a boil. Reduce the heat to a simmer and cook, covered and undisturbed, until the rice is just tender, about 20 to 25 minutes. Check the rice for doneness in several places.

(recipe continued at left)

Café Reconcile
CRAWFISH BISQUE

Café Reconcile's program has transformed the lives of nearly 1,000 at-risk young adults through work in the restaurant. When students graduate from the program they are prepped to successfully begin careers in the hospitality industries. The Emeril Lagasse Foundation is a major supporter, along with many other generous benefactors.

SERVES 8

FOR THE STUFFED CRAWFISH
1/2 cup vegetable oil (or unsalted butter)
2 cups minced onion
2 stalks celery, chopped
2 medium green bell peppers, seeded and minced
3 cloves garlic, minced
1/4 cup crawfish fat (or unsalted butter)
3/4 pound crawfish tails, peeled
4 to 5 slices day-old bread, soaked in water and squeezed dry
1/2 tablespoon salt
1 tablespoon freshly ground black pepper
1/2 tablespoon cayenne pepper
75 crawfish heads, cleaned
1/2 cup unseasoned breadcrumbs
1/2 cup seasoned breadcrumbs

Make the Stuffed Crawfish

1. In a large, heavy pot over medium heat, warm 1/4 cup of the oil and in it sauté the onion, celery, bell pepper, and garlic for 8 to 10 minutes, or until they are soft and golden. Add the crawfish fat and cook, stirring, for about 3 minutes, or until it is completely incorporated. Turn off the heat.

2. In a meat grinder or food processor, grind 1/2 pound of the crawfish tails with the moist bread and add the bread mixture to the vegetables. Turn the heat back on to medium.

3. In a large, heavy pot heat the remaining 1/4 cup oil over medium heat and add the bread/vegetable mixture, salt, black pepper, cayenne, and the remaining crawfish tails. Cook the stuffing mixture, stirring, for 5 to 8 minutes, remove it from the heat, and let it cool, stirring occasionally, to room temperature.

4. Preheat the oven to 375 degrees. In a small bowl mix together the unseasoned and seasoned breadcrumbs.

5. Stuff each crawfish head with about 1 tablespoon of the stuffing mixture, packing the breadcrumbs to adhere to the stuffing. Bake for about 15 to 20 minutes, or until lightly golden brown.

FOR THE BISQUE
1 tablespoon butter
1 tablespoon all-purpose flour
1 cup diced tomatoes
1/2 cup diced onion
1/4 cup diced celery
1 pound crawfish tails, whole and with fat*
1 bunch of scallions, chopped
1 quart heavy cream**
1/2 cup chicken stock
1 tablespoon Creole Seasoning (see page XX)
1 teaspoon Italian seasoning
cooked white rice to serve 8

*A little butter can replace the crawfish fat but you'll lose that flavor.
**Using cream is optional. Simply replace it with chicken, shrimp or seafood stock.

Make the Bisque

1. Make a roux; in a small saucepan over medium heat melt the butter. Whisk in the flour, being careful not to let clumps form, and continue to cook, stirring frequently, for about 25 to 30 minutes, or until a dark brown color is reached. Remove from the heat and set aside.

2. In a large saucepan over medium heat combine the tomatoes, onion, and celery, and cook for about 10 minutes, or until they begin to turn translucent. Add the crawfish tails and scallions and continue cooking for another 5 minutes.

3. Stir in the cream, stock, Creole Seasoning, and Italian seasoning. Bring to a boil and whisk in the roux. Reduce the heat to medium low and simmer for 20 minutes. Serve over white rice with the stuffed crawfish heads placed on top.

Chef Jeremy Langlois, Houmas House Plantation

CRAWFISH ÉTOUFFÉE

Common to both Creole and Cajun cuisines, étouffée are smothered dishes— cooked under a tight-fitting lid over low heat — traditionally served over rice. Chef Jeremy Langlois' addition of tomato to the dish put this version solidly in the Creole class.

SERVES 4

4 tablespoons butter
1 cup diced onions
1/2 cup diced bell pepper
2 tablespoons minced garlic
3 tablespoons all-purpose flour
1 pound peeled crawfish tail meat with fat*
2 cups crawfish stock or water
1 cup diced tomatoes
2 tablespoons chopped parsley
1 tablespoon cayenne pepper
salt and freshly ground black pepper to taste
4 cups cooked rice to serve

A little butter can replace the crawfish fat but you'll lose that flavor.

1. In a heavy-bottom pot over medium-high heat melt the butter and in it sauté the onion, bell pepper, and garlic for about 10 minutes, or until tender. Add the flour, stirring constantly and breaking up any lumps that form with a whisk to form a blond roux.

2. Add the crawfish, stock, and tomatoes, bring to a simmer, and cook, uncovered, for 30 minutes. Gently fold in the parsley, season to taste with the cayenne, salt, and pepper, and serve the étouffée over the steamed rice.

Chef Tommy DiGiovanni, Arnaud's

TROUT MEUNIÈRE

Arnaud's rich Meunière Sauce differs quite a bit from most others in that it begins with a base of sautéed aromatics and is enriched with both veal stock and roux.

SERVES 6

1 cup all-purpose flour
kosher salt and freshly ground black pepper to taste
1/2 cup whole milk
1/4 cup buttermilk
vegetable oil for frying
6 skinless trout fillets, preferably speckled trout, each 6 to 7 ounces
2 lemons, cut into wedges
parsley for garnish
1 recipe Meunière Sauce

1. In a large shallow bowl season the flour generously with salt and pepper and in another similar bowl combine the whole milk and buttermilk. In an electric fryer or heavy-bottomed saucepan heat the oil to 350 degrees. Line a baking sheet with several layers of paper towels and place in a warm oven.

2. Dredge two of the trout fillets in the flour, the milk mixture, and then the flour again, shaking off any excess, and lower them gently into the heated oil. Cook for 4 to 5 minutes, or until golden brown. Allow the oil to reheat before frying the next pair of fillets. Transfer the trout with a skimmer or slotted spoon to the lined baking sheet to keep them warm.

3. When all the fillets are cooked, transfer them to a serving platter and garnish them with the lemon wedges and parsley. Serve immediately with very warm Meunière Sauce.

MEUNIÈRE SAUCE

MAKES about 2 cups

2 tablespoons unsalted butter
1/2 stalk celery, finely chopped
1/2 white onion, finely chopped
1/4 cup finely chopped green bell pepper
1/4 cup finely chopped flat-leaf parsley
1/4 teaspoon freshly ground black pepper
1 Bouquet Garni (*see page 9*)
1 clove
1 1/2 cups Veal Stock
juice of 1/2 lemon
3 tablespoons medium-dark Roux (*see page 88*)
kosher salt and freshly ground black pepper to taste

(recipe continued at right)

Speckled trout are found throughout the shorelines of the Gulf of Mexico and bay areas. The shape, taste, and texture of speckled trout are ideal for many Creole recipes, making it the go-to finfish in New Orleans' upscale restaurants.

Arnaud's, in the historic French Quarter, is a leader of the culinary old guard, encompassing 14 historic buildings.

In 1918, a French wine salesman, Arnaud Cazenave, founded the grand restaurant that still bears his name. It opened just as the heyday of dining out exploded and is one of the few thriving Creole originals.

In 1979 Archie and Jane Casbarian refurbished the beautiful old restaurant, preparing it for another century of grandeur.

(recipe continued from left)

1. In a small saucepan melt the butter over high heat and add the celery, onion, bell pepper, parsley, black pepper, bouquet garni, and clove. Sauté, stirring occasionally, until nicely browned, about 4 minutes. Add the veal stock and lemon juice and bring to a boil. Boil the mixture for about 2 minutes, reduce the heat to a simmer, and cook for 10 minutes.

2. Add the roux, one tablespoon at a time, being sure to fully incorporate it before adding the next tablespoon, and season with the kosher salt and pepper to taste. Strain the sauce through a sieve over a bowl, pressing the solids to extract all the liquid, and discard the solids. Serve the sauce warm.

"How ya like dem ersters?" asked New Orleans' Mayor Robert Maestri at Antoine's as he and President Franklin Roosevelt dined on Oysters Rockefeller.

Antoine's created Oysters Rockefeller, their long-standing secret recipe, which absolutely does not contain spinach. Brennan's chefs produced their versions, also without spinach. Most restaurants include spinach as one of the green ingredients.

The rich creation by Jules Alciatore was named for John D. Rockefeller, for the man, who at the time, was considered the wealthiest in America.

If you would like to include spinach, reduce the amount of greens and toss in an equal handful of spinach leaves. Add a splash of Absinthe, Herbsaint, or Pernod for a hint of licorice flavor. It's hard to go wrong.

(recipe continued from right)

3. Preheat the oven to 400 degrees. Fill each of the baking dishes to just below their rim with the rock salt. Return the poached oysters to their shells, and place six shells in each baking dish.

4. Spoon about 1 1/2 tablespoons of the Rockefeller Sauce over each oyster and bake for about 12 minutes, or until the sauce is bubbly and begins to brown. Serve immediately, being sure to warn your guests about the hot dishes.

Note: Take care to remove all the parsley stems to avoid a resulting bitter taste. Similarly, take care to remove all the string from the celery to avoid a stringy texture in the sauce, and if using spinach, remove any tough stems.

Chef Robert Barker
OYSTERS ROCKEFELLER

SERVES 6

FOR THE OYSTERS
3 cups oyster liquor
1/2 teaspoon salt
juice of 1 lemon
3 dozen shucked oysters on the half shell

FOR THE ROCKEFELLER SAUCE
4 tablespoons (1/2 stick) butter
4 tablespoons all-purpose flour
2 bunches of parsley, stems removed completely, finely minced
2 bunches of scallions, green part only, finely minced
4 tablespoons tomato paste
8 ribs celery, strings removed completely, finely minced
1 1/2 tablespoons sugar
1 tablespoon white vinegar
1 tablespoon salt
1 teaspoon ground white pepper
1/2 teaspoon cayenne pepper
1/2 cup breadcrumbs
several cups of rock salt for bed

Prepare the Oysters

1. In a large saucepan heat the oyster liquor, salt, and lemon juice over medium-low heat and in it poach the oysters (do not discard their shells) for 1 to 2 minutes, or until their edges just barely curl.

2. Using a slotted spoon or tongs, transfer the oysters to a plate and set aside. Reserve 1 cup of the oyster liquor mixture and discard the rest.

Make the Rockefeller Sauce

1. In a large, heavy-bottom saucepan over medium heat melt the butter and stir in the flour, stirring constantly and making sure to break up any lumps, for about 2 minutes. Stir in the reserved oyster liquor, the parsley, scallions, tomato paste, celery, sugar, vinegar, salt, white pepper, and cayenne, until the mixture is blended well.

2. Reduce the heat to low, simmer, stirring occasionally, for 1 hour and 15 minutes, and stir in the breadcrumbs. Adjust the seasoning to taste just before use.

(recipe continued at left)

CJ Gerdes, Casamento's
OYSTER SOUP

Oysters thrive in water that is neither fresh nor salty, making Louisiana's brackish coastal waters particularly fertile grounds for the development of plump, glistening specimens. As the waters cool at the end of the year, oysters grow plump and salty.

SERVES 4 to 6

3 1/2 cups water
2 dozen freshly shucked oysters, drained
1/2 cup chopped celery
1/2 cup chopped scallions
1/2 cup chopped onion
1/4 cup unsalted butter
1/2 teaspoon finely chopped garlic
1/8 teaspoon dried thyme
1/8 teaspoon ground red pepper
1 bay leaf
3/4 cup heavy whipping cream
2 cups whole milk
1/2 cup all-purpose flour
1 teaspoon kosher or sea salt
1/4 teaspoon ground white pepper

1. In a medium saucepan bring the water to a boil. Add the oysters and cook for 3 minutes. Remove oysters with a slotted spoon and reserve 3 cups of liquid.

2. In a Dutch oven over medium heat, cook celery and onions in 1 tablespoon of butter, stirring constantly until tender. Stir in 2 1/2 cups of the reserved liquid, garlic, thyme, red pepper and bay leaf; bring to a boil. Stir in the cream. Reduce the heat and simmer 5 minutes. Stir in the milk and return to a simmer. Once the milk is added, never heat the soup past a simmer.

3. Melt the remaining butter in a small saucepan over low heat. Add the flour, stirring until smooth. Cook 1 minute, stirring constantly, then cook for about 3 more minutes until smooth (the mixture will be very thick).

4. Gradually add the flour mixture to the saucepan, stirring with a wire whisk until blended. Add oysters, salt and white pepper. Cook until thoroughly heated. Remove from heat, discard bay leaf and serve immediately.

Established by Joe Casamento, an immigrant from Ustica, Italy, the 1919 restaurant is tiled throughout. It continues as another of the city's long standing, favorite family owned and operated establishments.

Walls clad in blue and white ceramic tiles are a glistening backdrop for Casamento's oysters, more oysters, and other seafood in a variety of guises. The old-fashioned restaurant in Uptown New Orleans maintains an ages-old operating schedule, closing from early to late summer.

Raw oysters here are so fresh you taste the Gulf of Mexico before you taste the oyster. Or maybe they're the same thing. Prepare your own cocktail sauce, at a table or the oyster bar, and then spend some appetite eating them on the half shell. You don't need a fork when a correctly shucked oyster will practically slide out of its shell and into your mouth all by itself.

Casamento's luxurious oyster soup and crisp oyster loaves are worth a special trip. The seafood is always so fresh that it could jump from its natural habitat right onto plates, if inclined. But we're happy to give the seafood a hand up.

CJ Gertes represents this generation of his family, happily shucking oysters at the oyster bar.

Antoine's early 1930s–1940s menu, reproduced in the front of this book, spells gumbo as gombo, not unusual for the times.

Gombo is the African term for okra, a frequent ingredient in gumbos.

Filé (ground sassafras leaves) is also used, a contribution from the Choctaw indians.

Okra and filé powder are both thickening agents therefore almost never used together in the same gumbo. Or gombo.

Marti Shambra was passionate about top hats and tall tales, holding forth on any manner of subjects — from design to designing escapades as an artist, attracting literati, the theater crowd, Quarterites, and media people. He adored delicious gossip and snacked on adversaries.

He ruled the Marti's, the eponymous French Quarter bistro, was the first to provide a snappy, late-night, casual hangout for the locals, one of whom was Tennessee Williams. A close neighbor, he was unnoticed or, at least, undisturbed by other guests. Marti's suited him.

Marti was far more interested in maintaining a salon than cooking, but he expected a excellent, well prepared menu. He wisely installed his family's long-time hunting camp cook in the kitchen and left him to create magic. In return, Marti's served wonderful food. Chef Henry Robinson presented solid Creole fare in it's down-home goodness. There was nothing tricky, nothing fancy, nothing tortured into unnatural culinary acts.

Following Marti's too-early passing in 1988, the bistro was renamed Peristyle, after the bar's mural of City Park, circa 1911, from the old DeSoto Hotel. The restaurant then became Wolfe's, finally shuttering in 2009.

Patrick Singley, one of New Orleans' renowned restaurateurs, refreshed and resurrected Marti's in 2013, breathing new life into the storied corner.

Marti Shambra, Marti's
FILÉ GUMBO

Gumbo is always served over rice. In fact, with a salad and hot French bread, there's no more satisfying meal.

SERVES 4 to 6

4 tablespoons vegetable oil
1/2 pound raw ham, medium diced
1 pound small to medium shrimp
3 tablespoons all-purpose flour
1 small green bell pepper, roughly chopped
1 large onion, roughly chopped
4 celery stalks, roughly chopped
1 1/2 quarts chicken stock
1 dozen gumbo crabs*
1 cup raw chicken meat, medium-diced
or cut into small pieces
1 whole bay leaf
3 teaspoons filé powder
1 garlic clove, chopped
kosher or sea salt, to taste
freshly ground black pepper

Hard-shell crabs that are too small or scrawny to be picked for meat lumps are called gumbo crabs.

1. In a 5- or 6-quart Dutch oven (preferably made of cast iron) fry the ham and shrimp in the vegetable oil until the ham is a golden brown. Remove the ham and shrimp from the pot and set aside.

2. Add the flour to the remaining vegetable oil to begin making a roux *(see p.88)* constantly stirring and blending the flour and oil until the flour reaches a medium to dark brown color. Just before the roux's color reaches that point, stir the chopped onion, bell pepper and celery into the roux and cook them until the vegetable pieces become soft and semi-transparent, 5 to 10 minutes.

3. Add the chicken stock, crabs, shrimp, ham and diced chicken to the pot, as well as the bay leaf and chopped garlic. Cook on low-to-medium heat until the liquid is reduced to about 1 1/2 quarts.

4. Season to taste with salt and pepper. Just before serving, stir in the filé powder. Serve over cooked rice.

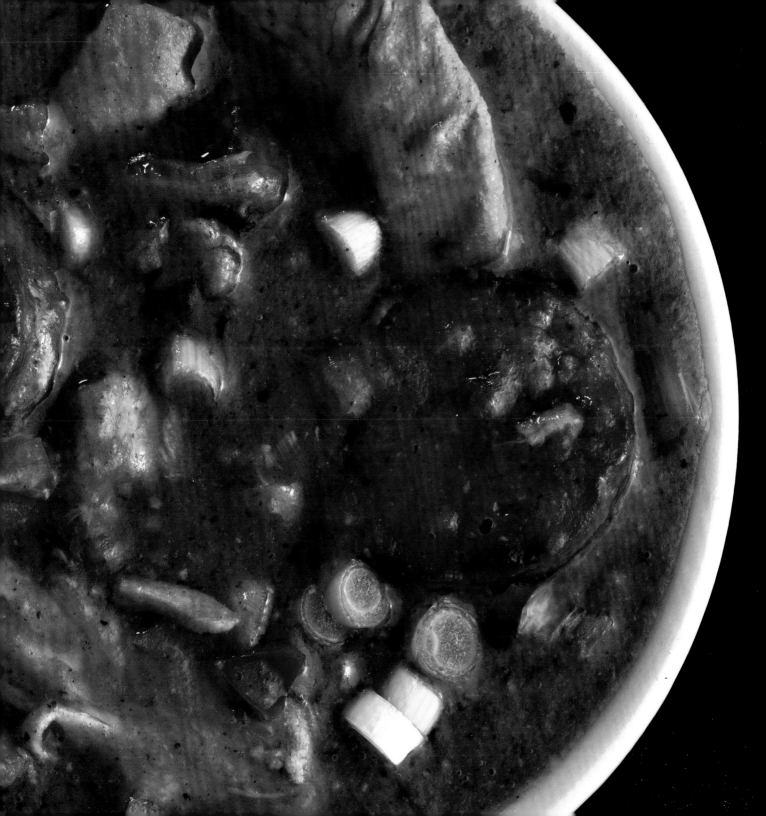

Chef Robert Barker
FAMILY GUMBO

There's not much more satisfying than a group of family and friends around a big pot of gumbo. This is chef Robert's basic gumbo recipe, ready for personal tweaking.

SERVES 8 to 10

4 sticks unsalted butter, melted, or 2 cups olive oil
2 cups all-purpose flour
1 red bell pepper, diced
1 green bell pepper, diced
2 medium yellow onions, diced
2 stalks celery, diced
4 quarts Poultry Stock, heated
1 can of amber beer
2 tablespoons Creole Seasoning (*see page 67*)
1 teaspoon freshly ground black pepper
1 teaspoon crushed red pepper
1 teaspoon chili powder
1 teaspoon thyme
1 tablespoon chopped garlic
2 bay leaves
kosher salt to taste
1 pound andouille, or smoked sausage, sliced 1/2-inch thick
3 to 4 pounds chicken or turkey roasted, deboned, and cut into, cut into 2-inch pieces
Louisiana hot sauce to taste

1. First make a roux (*see page 88.*) Heat the butter or oil in a large stockpot or dutch oven. Whisk in the flour and cook until foaming. Cook, stirring often, until the roux is a dark mahogany color, about 1 hour.

2. Add the peppers, onion, and celery (*see page 90 for the "trinity"*) and cook until translucent, about 5 minutes. Heat, then whisk in the hot poultry stock and beer, and bring the mixture to a boil. Reduce the heat to a simmer, and stir in the Creole Seasoning, black pepper, crushed red pepper, chili powder, thyme, chopped garlic, bay leaves, and kosher salt. Cook, skimming off the fat as necessary, an additional 45 minutes.

3. In a skillet, brown the sausage and drain. Add the sausage and chicken or turkey to the stockpot, adjust the seasonings, and serve the gumbo over cooked white rice.

Chef Robert always called this "family gumbo" because he made it after holiday events when turkey and other poultry carcasses were abundant.

These carcasses are used as the base for a flavorful, rich stock. Any leftover meat — ducks, and chicken — in addition to turkey from the feast may be added.

POULTRY STOCK

MAKES 1 gallon

4 quarts of cold water
2 pounds of any combination of poultry carcasses and trimmings
2 medium yellow onions, chopped
2 large leeks, white and green parts cut in half lengthwise and well washed
2 celery stalks, including tops, chopped
4 bay leaves
1 teaspoon dried thyme
1 1/2 teaspoons whole white peppercorns
1 whole garlic head, the cloves peeled and crushed

1. In a large stockpot bring 4 quarts of water with all the other ingredients to a low boil. Reduce the heat and simmer, partially covered, for 45 minutes, skimming off any impurities that rise to the top.

2. Strain out all the solids, discarding them, and allow the stock to cool. Any stock not to be used immediately will keep in several smaller airtight containers in the refrigerator for up to 5 days or frozen.

Monday in New Orleans is to red beans and laundry as Monday in Boston is to baked beans and laundry. We serve red beans and rice alongside fried chicken, hot or andouille sausage, or pork chops. The beans have been simmered with ham bones and slow cooked for hours.

We like to prepare a double recipe and freeze half.

Any leftover red beans, should there ever be such a thing, can create a rich soup when mashed, chicken stock added, warmed, and topped with finely chopped onion, shredded Cheddar cheese, and browned, sliced sausage.

Red beans also anchor an especially delicious omelet dressed with cheese, onions, and sliced sausage.

Louis "Satchmo" Armstrong signed his letters "Red Beans and Ricely Yours," in an affectionate nod to his hometown. We return the favor each year and celebrate Satchmo Fest in the French Quarter. When fans fly in, they touch down at the Louis "Satchmo" Armstrong airport.

Remoulade is a handsome antique oyster bar that celebrates fresh Louisiana seafood along with a fine selection of local dishes. Next door to Arnaud's, the café stands as the grande dame's nod to casual Creole cooking.

While New Orleanians dine extravagantly on occasion, we also relish a great plate of jambalaya, red beans and rice, gumbo, fresh seafood, and other recipes traditionally stirred up in local kitchens.

Remoulade is named in honor of Arnaud's famous sauce and offers a few of its big sister's specialties.

The exposed brick reminds us that it is one of the French Quarter's original Creole homes.

Archie Casbarian, Remoulade
RED BEANS *and* RICE

This recipe is subject to as many interpretations as there are Creole cooks. Some cooks soak the beans overnight, some do not soak at all. Soaking decreases the cooking time. Red beans freeze very well, so save any leftovers.

SERVES 10 to 12

2 pounds dried red beans, rinsed and soaked overnight
2 smoked ham hocks
1 bottle Abita Amber or similar beer
1 white or yellow onion, chopped
1 green bell pepper, chopped
2 stalks celery, chopped
1/2 cup chopped parsley
10 cloves garlic, finely diced
1 teaspoon dried oregano
2 teaspoons dried thyme
4 bay leaves
2 tablespoons Worcestershire sauce
2 tablespoons liquid smoke
3-inch cinnamon stick
1 teaspoon freshly ground black pepper
1 teaspoon white pepper
1/2 teaspoon cayenne pepper
two 2-inch pieces of salt pork, blanched for 5 minutes in boiling water
1 pound smoked sausage, such as andouille, smoked sausage, or Kielbasa, cut into 3-inch rounds
cooked white rice for serving

1. In a large stockpot, combine the beans, ham hocks, beer, vegetables, herbs, seasonings, and salt pork. Add one gallon of water to the pot (add more if the water does not cover the ingredients by at least 2 inches) and bring the water to a boil. Reduce the heat to a simmer and cook for 3 hours.

2. In a frying pan, brown the sausage and add to the finished red beans.

3. If you want a creamier texture, scoop out some of the beans using a slotted spoon, mash them, and return them to the pot. Cook the bean mixture for an additional 15 minutes and serve it over cooked white rice, heated, in shallow bowls.

Chef Robert Bruce, Maylie's
DEVILED EGGS

Maylie's deviled eggs with Remoulade Sauce is one of those mystical recipes so well remembered by patrons of the legendary establishment. They seem to be the first to drizzle their signature Rémoulade Sauce over deviled eggs. Maylie's Remoulade Sauce recipe sets itself apart by using pickle relish as a sweet, yet still tangy ingredient. Chef Bruce provided this authentic recipe.

MAKES 2 Dozen Eggs, 48 halves

2 dozen eggs, jumbo, at room temperature
1 cup sweet pickle relish, drained
1 cup mayonnaise
paprika for garnish
scallion tops for garnish

To Make the Eggs

1. Place eggs in a pot of cool water just covering the eggs and bring to a boil. Remove pan from heat and allow eggs to sit in water for 10 minutes. Remove from water and let cool in pot under cold running water for 2 minutes, drain.

2. Roll eggs on cutting board gently and crush the shells lightly. Remove the shell in a bath of water and place peeled eggs on a dry clean towel to dry. With a sharp thin knife, slice eggs, long ways in half and allow egg to rest on its white with yolk facing up.

3. Gently remove yolk with teaspoon and place yolk in mixing bowl with mayonnaise and relish. Mash well with a fork. Place egg halves in appropriate container and using a pastry bag with star tip, fill all eggs. The Maylie's way was to mound the stuffing in each egg half and smooth using the tines of a fork before dressing with Rémoulade Sauce and garnish.

Closing on New Year's Eve 1986, Maylie's became a Smith & Wollensky's, and is now in another restaurant incarnation. Maylie's was the city's second or third oldest restaurant, opening in 1876 to serve working men from the nearby market a hearty meal, as so many other restaurants began.

Family always operated Maylie's and lived over the restaurant. Their culinary tradition continues through chef Robert Bruce, who spent his youth in Maylie's kitchen with his family.

Chef Bruce became Smith & Wollensky's chef, Maylie's former home, having previously established a name for himself at other outstanding New Orleans establishments.

Author Tom Fitzmorris says that Maylie's six-course table d'hote dinner at the end was $6.50:

Deviled eggs remoulade
Soup of the day
Salad
Fish course
Boiled beef brisket with potatoes
Bread pudding

Willie's
REMOULADE SAUCE
MAKES about 1 cup

1/3 cup Creole mustard
2 tablespoons white vinegar
2 scallions, minced
1 teaspoon chopped garlic
2 tablespoons ketchup
2 ounces extra virgin olive oil

Make the Remoulade Sauce

Combine the mustard, vinegar, scallions, garlic, and ketchup in a small food processor. With the processor running, slowly drizzle the olive oil in until it is totally emulsified. Refrigerate in a closed container for at least an hour prior to serving.

Like most dishes of humble origins, Dirty Rice owes its existence to the original cooks, who simply made the most of what was on hand. A frugal cook would finely mince the chicken liver, heart, and gizzard; mix them with rice; and season with the ever-present "Holy Trinity" (onion, bell pepper, and celery) of Louisiana cooking. The flavorful, one-pot meal cooked quickly and fed a family on the cheap. The browned bits of meat give the white rice a "dirty" look, hence the name.

Variations include using ground sausage, beef, or other meats in place of the ground organ meats. Today it is also more commonly served as a side dish to grilled or fried meats instead of starring as the main attraction.

Chef Emeril Lagasse shook up the culinary world, resulting in increased recognition for New Orleans, and our legacy of great restaurants. While his restaurant empire ranges across the country, his background, and home base operations here, are matters of local pride. I've always wanted to call it home plate but that's a personal opinion. He's given back to the city much more than great food, and is a hometown hero.

His tour as Executive Chef with Commander's Palace gave him an appetite for adventure. When he christened Emeril's, the restaurant world rocked while he rolled. His books and television series have helped to teach cooks to view food as entertainment, no matter where it is prepared. In New Orleans, Emeril's, Delmonico, and NOLA showcase his talent.

He made New Orleans his own, using creativity, a sense of humor, and a big heart. Emeril has mentored an increasing number of talented chefs, who continue to cook here and elsewhere.

Civic and community activities are generous and far-reaching, including the Emeril Lagasse Foundation.

Emeril Lagasse, Emeril's
DIRTY RICE

Chicken or turkey livers and giblets may be used in place of more costly duck livers for this dish. However, when using the heart and gizzard in addition to the liver, both should be finely ground in order to avoid a chewy texture.

SERVES 8 to 12 sides

3 tablespoons vegetable oil
1 pound finely chopped chicken or duck livers
1/2 pound pork sausage, removed from casings and crumbled
1 cup finely chopped yellow onion
3/4 cup finely chopped green bell pepper
1/4 cup finely chopped celery
2 teaspoons minced garlic
1 tablespoon Creole Seasoning (see page 67)
1 teaspoon salt
1 teaspoon freshly ground black pepper
2 cups chicken stock
2 bay leaves
5 cups cooked rice, chilled
1/4 cup minced fresh parsley

1. In a large heavy saucepan over medium-high heat, heat 2 tablespoons of the vegetable oil and in it sauté the livers and sausage for about 6 minutes, or until the meat is browned. Add the remaining tablespoon oil, the onion, bell pepper, celery, garlic, Creole seasoning, salt, and black pepper and cook until the vegetables have softened, about 5 minutes.

2. Add the stock and bay leaves, scraping the bottom of the pan to release any browned bits. Bring to a boil, reduce the heat to a simmer, and cook for 5 minutes. Fold in the cooked rice and heat through, about 5 minutes. Remove from the heat and remove the bay leaves. Stir in the parsley, or simply sprinkle it over the rice, and serve immediately.

Jyl Benson
OYSTER DRESSING

This recipe calls for margarine. Do not substitute butter. Double, triple, or quadruple the recipe as necessary to service the holiday feast. It freezes beautifully, so don't hesitate to make enough to save for another event.

SERVES 6 to 8

20 small Louisiana oysters, shucked, with their liquor
1 cup cold water
8 tablespoons (1 stick) margarine
1 1/2 cups chopped onions
1 cup chopped celery
1 cup chopped green bell pepper
3 bay leaves
1 recipe Jyl's Creole Spice mix (at right)
1 teaspoon minced garlic
1 to 2 cups Italian breadcrumbs
2 tablespoons unsalted butter, at room temperature
1/4 cup chopped scallions

1. Combine the oysters, liquor, and water in a medium sized bowl, cover and refrigerate for one hour. Strain the oysters out of the liquor and water. Reserve the oysters and liquid in separate containers in the fridge until ready to use.

2. Preheat oven to 350 degrees. In a large skillet (preferably cast iron) melt 4 tablespoons of the margarine over high heat, add half the onions, celery, bell pepper, the bay leaves, and cook, stirring frequently, until the onions are browned, about 8 minutes. Add 2 tablespoons of the spice mix and the garlic, reduce the heat to medium, and cook another 5 minutes.

3. Add the remaining half onion, celery, and bell pepper, stir in the remaining margarine and the bay leaves, and cook for 10 minutes, stirring occasionally. Turn the heat to high and fold in the oysters and their liquid. Cook for another 10 minutes.

4. Fold in the remaining spice mixture and enough breadcrumbs to thicken. Transfer to an ungreased, 8-inch square baking dish and bake for 30 minutes, or until the top has lightly browned. Fold in the butter and chopped scallions. Serve immediately.

Thanksgiving brings heightened demand for Louisiana oyster producers, and Sal Sunseri, proprietor of New Orleans' P&J Oysters, says he always sells out to celebrants for whom it wouldn't be Thanksgiving without the savory shellfish dressing.

Oyster liquor is pure gold. A small amount of clear liquid remains with the oyster in the bottom half shell when it is properly and carefully shucked. We harvest this liquor for flavor by draining and straining it for use in any manner of oyster recipes, or slurp when we're eating raw oysters on the half shell.

Jyl is a celebrated author and one of Louisiana and the South's foremost culinary authorities.

CREOLE SEASONING MIX

You may double, triple, or quadruple this recipe and store the remainder in small covered jars. They also make terrific gifts.

1/2 teaspoon salt
1/2 teaspoon cayenne pepper
1/2 teaspoon sweet paprika
1/2 teaspoon ground black pepper
1/2 teaspoon onion powder
1/2 teaspoon dried oregano
1/2 teaspoon dried thyme

In a small bowl combine the salt, Cayenne, paprika, black pepper, onion powder, oregano, and thyme.

Chef Chris Lynch, Café Atchafalaya
COLLARD GREENS

Collard green are served as a side with Café Atchafalaya's cane glazed quail. They are a delicious accompaniment to almost any entree.

SERVES 6 to 8

3 slices of thick-cut bacon, sliced
1/2 onion, finely julienned
4 cloves garlic, finely diced
3 bunches of collard greens, stemmed, ripped into thirds, and rinsed
1 bottle amber beer
1 tablespoon Worcestershire sauce
2 tablespoons Crystal Hot Sauce
1/3 cup Steen's Cane Syrup
1/2 gallon water

1. In a heavy-bottomed stockpot render the bacon over medium heat for 3 minutes. Add the onion and garlic and cook for 8 to 10 minutes, or until they are golden. Add the collard greens, pour the beer over the greens, and cook for 5 to 10 minutes, or until the beer has reduced by half.

2. Add the Worcestershire sauce, Crystal, Steen's, and enough water to cover all the ingredients. Reduce the heat to low and simmer, covered, for 1 1/2 to 2 hours, adding more water if the greens begin to dry.

Chef Chris Lynch, Café Atchafalaya
OKRA TOMATO STEW

Okra tomato stew dances beside the collard greens and cane glazed quail but also may be served with various entrees.

SERVES 6 to 8

1/4 pound tasso ham, cut into 1/4-inch cubes
1/2 onion, diced
1 green bell pepper, diced
3 stalks celery, diced
1/2 pound green okra, sliced 1/4-inch thick
16-ounce can crushed tomatoes
3 tablespoons Crystal Hot Sauce
1 tablespoon Worcestershire sauce
1 tablespoon honey
1 quart chicken stock

1. In a medium pot over medium heat sauté the tasso, onion, bell pepper, celery, and okra for about 8 minutes, or until they just begin to brown.

2. Add the remaining ingredients, reduce the heat to a simmer, and cook, covered, for 40 minutes. Serve warm.

SWEETS

Sugarcane was one of the money crops in early Louisiana, grown on plantations and rapidly become an integral part of the south Louisiana economy and culture.

In 1751 Jesuit priests brought sugarcane into south Louisiana. Etienne de Bore harvested the first successful crop used to produce raw sugar in 1795. The thriving sugar industry quickly replaced the cultivation of indigo.

By the time of the Louisiana Purchase in 1803, Houmas House Plantation was established and producing sugar.

The plantation was also known as the Baron's Sugar Palace, once the country's largest sugar producer. In 1857 almost 100,000 acres of sugarcane were under cultivation. At the end of the 1800s, the plantation produced 20 million pounds of sugar annually, helping to lay the foundation for an industry that now contributes $2 billion to the Louisiana economy.

Then, bananas had their turn. The Standard Fruit Company was founded in 1899 by Italian immigrants in Plaquemines Parish after a freeze sent farmers to Central America for goods to sell in the French Market. Banana trees were planted. Less than a decade later, New Orleans was the nation's largest banana importer, a position it held for much of the century.

Native pecan trees were already sourced when New Orleans was settled. Native Indian tribes like the Attakapas, Caddos, Coushattas, and Houmas shared the sweet nuts with settlers. The pecan trees were then cultivated by the city's residents.

Creole cooks still take advantage of these crops, adding to an ever-expanding repertoire of good things to eat.

Ursuline Nuns
PRALINES

The crown jewel of New Orleans' confections, there are as many praline recipes as there are bread- pudding recipes. Everyone has a favorite. Sister Mary's pralines are fragile, sugary, and melt-in-your-mouth light.

MAKES about 5 dozen

1 pound light brown sugar
2 1/2 cups granulated sugar
2 1/2 cups whole milk
pinch of salt
2 1/2 cups chopped pecans
1/8 cup (1/4 stick) unsalted butter
1 teaspoon vanilla extract (or maple extract if desired)

1. In a medium-sized pot combine the sugars, milk, and salt and cook the mixture over medium heat, stirring frequently to avoid burning, until a candy thermometer reads 240 degrees. Remove the pot from heat to prevent scorching and using a long-handled spoon drop a small amount of the mixture into a bowl of cold water. The candy should form a soft, loose ball. If it doesn't, return it the pot, cook a short while longer, and test again.

2. Once the candy forms soft balls, turn the heat off and stir in the pecans, butter, and vanilla or maple extract. Let the candy cool in the pot for 10 minutes.

3. Stir the mixture until the consistency is right for spooning (50 to 100 strokes). Spoon tablespoon-sized dollops onto a marble slab or waxed paper to cool and dry. When the top is dry, lift each praline carefully using a spatula and turn it over to allow the bottom to dry as well. Store in a tightly covered container or wrap each praline individually.

Legend tells us that pralines were named after César du Plessis Praslin, a grand marshal of pre-Napoleonic France. It is said Praslin's cook, Clément Lassagne, coated his master's almonds with sugar to prevent indigestion.

As early settlers of New Orleans in the 1700s, nuns contributed mightily to the city's heritage and spiritual well-being.

They have provided cookery, medical care, gardening, education, and other charitable and religious services to the community. Nuns are credited with bringing the recipe for almond praline candy to New Orleans from France. Once here, they substituted the readily available pecans, as so many Creole recipes have evolved.

Sister Mary's version of the recipe has been passed down through generations of nuns. The candies could be appropriately pronounced pray-leens, but we say praw-leens, otherwise, us locals will know you're not from around here.

Today, in a cloistered convent surrounded by high brick walls and magnificent oak trees, the few remaining Poor Clare nuns share quiet, contemplative lives dedicated to poverty and prayer.

Sister Mary makes and sells pralines as her part of sustaining the order. Visitors simply ring the convent bell. Sometimes the candies are available. At other times, they are not.

Many an eighteenth-century New Orleans morning rang to the sound of female African American street vendors calling their wares as they ventured from the Treme neighborhood, where free people of color resided, to the French Quarter. Their heads topped with colorful tignons and bearing baskets of fried-rice boulles, or calas, they sang out "Calas! Calas, tout chaud!" The fried-rice boulles, or Calas, which they sold for pennies, were dusted with confectioners' sugar, honey, pancake syrup, or drizzled with Steen's cane syrup.

A time-honored treat in the Creole community, sweet calas may also be made savory by eliminating the sugar and adding seasonings and bits of leftover meat, such as ham.

Poppy Tooker
SWEET CALAS

Calas are best started with cold rice. Several-days-old white rice leftovers will work just fine. That's what the Creole cooks did, and it still makes perfect sense.

MAKES about 2 dozen

6 tablespoons all-purpose flour
4 tablespoons sugar
2 teaspoons baking powder
1/4 teaspoon salt
a pinch of nutmeg
2 cups cooked rice
2 large eggs, beaten
1/4 teaspoon vanilla
vegetable oil for frying
confectioners' sugar, honey, or Steen's Cane Syrup for topping

1. In a medium-sized bowl combine the flour, sugar, baking powder, salt, and nutmeg. In a separate bowl combine the rice, beaten eggs, and vanilla. Stir the dry ingredients into the egg mixture, taking care not to let clumps form.

2. In an electric fryer or heavy-bottomed skillet, bring the oil to 350 degrees. Carefully place teaspoon-sized clumps of the batter in the oil, in batches to prevent crowding and being careful not to splash the hot oil. Fry the calas until golden brown, turning them once, using tongs or a slotted spoon, to brown the other side.

3. Transfer each calas as it is cooked to a tray lined with paper towels to drain. Serve immediately, sprinkled with sugar or drizzled with the honey or syrup.

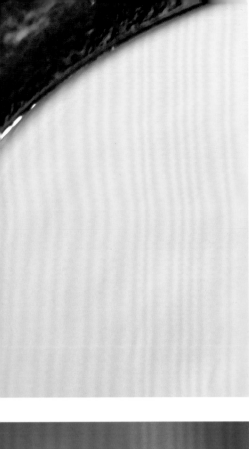

ROUX

Roux is the magical thickener and flavoring necessary for many gumbos, stews, and soups in Louisiana cooking. Making roux is not nearly as difficult as it may sound and can approach a Zen-like experience for a dedicated cook. Depending on skill and speed, creating a light ("blond") roux can take a few minutes and a dark roux up to 45 minutes to an hour.

The great news is that roux freezes beautifully. So make a large batch, cool it, then apportion it into small containers and freeze it for future use.

A roux is nothing more than flour browned in oil or fat, and it delivers much more flavor than that would suggest. The raw-flour taste is eliminated in the final product, and the chemical reaction created by the flour browning in the hot oil imparts a nutty, smoky flavor that deepens as the roux becomes darker. The scent as the reaction begins is distinctive and appetizing.

A Creole or Cajun roux begins with flour and oil or fat in equal proportions. Some cooks prefer a thicker roux, using more flour than oil. The language of roux pertains to its different hues, which can range from a barely colored tan to the color of peanut butter and through café au lait to dark mahogany. Before choosing the oil or fat, decide on the flavor and color of roux you're seeking. For example, a blond roux's flavor is more subtle but has higher thickening power than a dark roux.

The appropriate cooking medium is anything from vegetable oil, olive oil, or canola oil to bacon grease, Crisco, or lard. Butter burns easily at low temperatures, so unless it is clarified and the solids skimmed off, it will not work easily for a darker roux.

While white all-purpose flour is the norm, whole-wheat flour imparts a splendid nutty taste. The one-to-one ratio of oil and flour is standard, although some cooks prefer a bit more flour than oil, as much as 1/2 a cup flour on a one cup-to one-cup measurement.

Begin the process by turning on some music (for entertainment while you're stirring) and assembling the necessary equipment. The ideal basic tools are a comfortable wire whisk and a cast-iron skillet or Dutch oven. Thin metal pots significantly increase the risk of scorching.

Start the roux by heating the oil over medium-low heat. Add the flour slowly, stirring continuously with a whisk or a wooden spoon. Be patient and take your time. Once the oil and flour begin to emulsify and bubble, the heat level can be raised or lowered. But this calls for diligence. The color stays deceptively the same for some minutes, then changes rapidly. The flour can scorch before you're able to react. (There is no saving a scorched roux. It is over, it is finished, and it must be trashed.) Don't feel bad, it happens to us all.

Once the roux starts to approach the desired color level, remove it from the heat a shade or two lighter than you want to end up with and continue whisking, as the flour will continue to cook quickly and darken further.

The already-dark roux will continue to darken when the trinity is added and cooked, a cook's delicate balancing act.

TRINITY

If you intend to use the roux for gumbo, you'll want to add the "trinity" of Creole-Cajun cooking—chopped onion, celery, and bell pepper. While the addition of these vegetables will cause the roux to darken, it also begins cooling the roux as the vegetables cook and release their liquids. Once the vegetables have softened, gradually begin stirring in the warm stock or other liquid. Some chefs reverse the process, cooking the vegetables in the oil then adding the roux, and stock, or other liquid. The proportions among the trinity's components can vary according to the cook's fancy, as well as the cook's personal preferences among them and what happens to be in the refrigerator at a given moment. The trinity is:

2 parts onion, chopped
1 part celery, chopped
1 part green bell pepper, chopped

Many recipes call for bell peppers. Their confetti colors of green, yellow, red, and orange are bright, so use whichever one, or combination of them, you prefer.

Once the vegetables are chopped, combined, and set aside, prepare the roux. When the roux has been cooked to a shade or two under what you're seeking, carefully begin stirring in the trinity. When the vegetables hit the hot roux they will splatter, so add them slowly and stand back from the pot or skillet. When the vegetables have been completely incorporated into the roux, the flour will darken even more. Allow the mixture to simmer until the vegetables release their liquids and the onions are translucent.

At this point, slowly stir in the stock or water until well blended. Louisiana cookbook author Marcelle Bienvenu, whose vast experience makes her an expert in these matters, prefers to heat the liquid before adding it.

From the very beginning of the cooking process, the quality of the roux, trinity, and stock is most important for a gumbo's full-bodied flavor. A word of caution about seafood gumbo: Reserve the delicately flavored raw oysters, shrimp, fish, or crawfish until the gumbo is just a few minutes from being removed from the heat. Otherwise, the seafood will overcook, becoming tough and tasteless. The same applies to other proteins such as sausage, chicken, and duck. Give them enough time to cook at the end, but take care not to leech out their flavor by overcooking.

FRESH BOUQUET GARNI

"Bouquet garni" is the French term for a bundle of fresh herbs tied together and later tossed into the pot. After cooking it is then removed, using a slotted spoon, and discarded, so only the flavor of the seasonings remains in the dish.

Any appropriate herbs may be combined to make a bouquet garni. Tie the sprigs together with cooking twine and simply drop the little package in the pot. Many cooks tie one end of the sting to the pot's handle to make fishing out the bouquet garni a little easier.

Or, you can enclose herbs or dry seasonings in a 7-inch square of cheesecloth; draw the four corners together at the top, and tie into a little pouch, leaving enough string to tie to the handle.

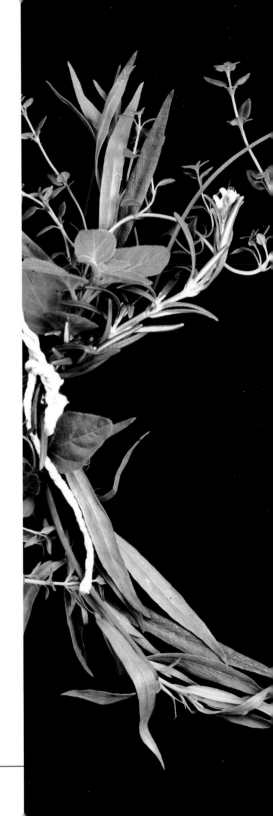

INDEX

French Market circa 1910

ACKNOWLEDGEMENTS

We adore our chefs and restaurateurs. No one is more generous and gracious. How did we secure recipes from these world-renowned chefs and famous restaurateurs? It was easy. We asked. I said they were generous. That's why they love to feed people.

My gratitude to our test kitchen and production commando, Barry Garner and chef Brandon Canizaro.

Appreciation is due in full measure to the creative talents of Elaine Richard, our sterling editor and Chris Rose, the brilliant writer; and the enduring patience of Michael Lauve, our art director. Photographer Sam Hanna worked with good humor, skill, and an abundance of talent. Paul Rico made his customary, brilliant contribution. Behind the scenes with welcome enthusiasm were stalwarts Scott Campbell, Terry Callaway, and Nina Kooij of Pelican Publishing.

Friends make the journey especially fulfilling, people such as Poppy Tooker, Jyl Benson, Grace Bauer, Rebecca Theim, and Linda Ellerbee. It's no surprise that they are each an accomplished author and freely share their expertise. No one could ask for such encouragement and moral support.

Billy, my husband, lightens my spirits and keeps us all laughing.

Any errors or omissions are purely my doing. If you have any questions or comments, I'd love to hear from you.

La Louisiane 719 Rue Iberville circa 1890

GALATOIRE'S

A LA CARTE SERVICE ONLY

To simplify your order, may we suggest:

APPETIZERS: Galatoire's Special or Martini..............50

HORS-D'oeuvres: Shrimp Remoulade.......................60

Oysters Rockfeller...1/2....60........doz.....1.20

SOUP: Soup of the Day................................25

FISH: Trout Marguery.....................1.00

Trout Amandine....................1.00

Pompano Amandine.................1.50

Egg: Eggs St Denis or Benedict...................75

CHICKEN: Chicken a la Rochambeau................1.25

SALAD: Mixed Green Salad......................30

DESSERT: Coupe Princesse......................50

Circa 1940s, during WWII, when much was rationed.

DUE TO SHORTAGE ONLY ONE PIECE OF BUTTER PER CUSTOMER

IF POSSIBLE

Specialitees de la Maison

Shrimp Arnaud 40	Canapé de Crab Pontchartrain 50
Filet de Truite Amandine 75	Canapé de Crab Pontchartrain
Supreme de Volaille en Papillote . . . 1.00	avec Anchois 60
Stuffed Crab Rejane (Cold) 50	Chicken Coquille à la Reine 75
Poulet Saute Clemenceau . . . . (½) 1.25	Bouillabaisse de Pompano
Langouste Sarah Bernhardt . . . (½) 1.00	Madelon (for two) 2.50
Brochette de Filet Mignon Richelieu . . 1.00	Poulet Sauté "Bostonian" 1.25
Salad Faucon 30	Stuffed Turkey Wing, Marquise 75
Banane Flambée Surprise 75	Cotelettes d'agneau Mirabeau 1.25
	Jeune coq au Porto 1.25
	Crepe Suzette Arnaud 75

Hors-D'Oeuvres

(Whet the appetite, like a long walk when the air is crisp and tangy.)

Pickles or Olives 15	Avocado Romanoff (in season) 85
Pickled White Onions 25	Crab Canapé 50
Queen Olives 25	Crab Canapé with Anchovies 60
Ripe Olives 25	Stuffed Crab Rejane (cold) 50
Stuffed Olives 30	Canapé Savarin 60
Pickled Walnuts (3) 30	Fruit Cocktail 40
Celery, Plain 30	Canapé of Caviar (Imported Beluga) . .80
Celery, Stuffed, Roquefort Cheese 60	Paté de Foie Gras en Terrine 60
Shrimp Arnaud 40	Grilled Sardines on Anchovy Toast . . .60
Anti Pasto, per tin 50	Grape Fruit Mikado 50
Imported Sardines, per tin 50	Canapé Capucine 50
Croquettes Richelieu 60	Fonds d'Artichaut à la Russe 85
Allumettes aux Anchois Victoria	Canapé of Anchovies 40
(2 persons or 3 persons) 1.20	Tomato à l'Imperiale 50
Avocado Cocktail (in season) 25	

Oysters

Oysters, Raw on Half Shell . (½ doz.) .30	Oysters, Rockefeller . . . . (½ doz.) .50
Stewed in Milk . . " .30	A l'Americaine . . " .60
Stewed in Cream . . " .35	Suzette . . . . . " .50
Fried, Plain . . . " .30	Roasted with Bacon . " .40
Fried in Butter . . " .40	Lucullus . . . . . " .90
Brochette . . . . " .50	Scalloped or Pan Roast " .40
Broiled on Toast . . " .30	Marinière (dozen) .85
A la Créole . . . " .50	Poulette 90
En Coquille à la Reine " .60	Patties (2) 90

Potages

Soup du Jour 15	Créole Gumbo 30
Consommé, Hot or Frappé 20	Turtle 25
A la Reine 25	Cream of Tomato or Asparagus 30
Potage Paysanne 30	Onion Soup, Gratin, Plain 30
Oyster Soup, Plain . .(½ doz. Oysters) .35	Cream .35
Cream 40	Crayfish Bisque Evelyn (in season) . . .30

Poissons

Filet de Truite, Meuniére 60	Flounder, Broiled 65
Colbert 75	Meuniére 70
Amandine 75	Colbert 80
Marguery 85	Pompano, Broiled 85
Broiled 50	Meuniére 90
Fried, Tartar Sauce . . .50	Papillote 1.00
Filet of Red Fish, Broiled or Fried, Tartar	Pontchartrain 1.25
Sauce 50	Sheephead, Broiled 60
Court-bouillon . . .85	Meuniére 65
Gratin 90	Hollandaise 75
Spanish Mackerel, Broiled 60	Gratin 90
Matelotte 75	Red Snapper, Chambord (4 or 6 persons)
Fish Coquille à la Reine 50	(1 day's notice) 6.00
Pressed Cold Fish, Ravigote 40	($1.00 for each added person)
	Bouillabaisse, Prado 1.00

ARNAUD'S